on

being

a

therapist

REVISED
EDITION

JEFFREY A. KOTTLER

on

being

a

therapist

REVISED
EDITION

Jossey-Bass Publishers
San Francisco

Substantial discounts on bulk quantities of Jossey-Bass books are available to corporations, professional associations, and other organizations. For details and discount information, contact the special sales department at Jossey-Bass Inc., Publishers. (415) 433-1740; Fax (415) 433-0499.

For sales outside the United States, contact Maxwell Macmillan International Publishing Group, 866 Third Avenue, New York, New York 10022.

Manufactured in the United States of America

Library of Congress Cataloging-in-Publication Data

Kottler, Jeffrey A.
    On being a therapist / Jeffrey A. Kottler. — Rev. ed.
       p. cm. — (The Jossey-Bass social and behavioral science series)
    Includes bibliographical references and index.
    ISBN 1-55542-555-0 (alk. paper)
    1. Psychotherapists — Psychology. 2. Psychotherapy — Practice — Psychological aspects. 3. Psychotherapist and patient. I. Title. II. Series.
    [DNLM: 1. Professional Practice. 2. Physician-Patient Relations. 3. Psychotherapy. WM 21 K87o 1993]
    RC480.5.K68   1993
    616.89′14′023 — dc20
    DNLM/DLC
    for Library of Congress   93-15864
                                               CIP

REVISED EDITION
PB Printing   10 9 8 7 6 5 4 3 2   *Code 9382*

The
Jossey-Bass
Social and Behavioral
Science Series

contents

preface

*t*he process of psychotherapy flows in two directions, obviously influencing the client but also affecting the personal life of the clinician. This impact can be for better or for worse, making the helping professions among the most spiritually fulfilling as well as the most emotionally draining human endeavors. Some of us flourish as a result of this work. We learn from those we try to help and apply what we know and understand to ourselves. And some of us become depleted and despondent. Over time we may become cynical or indifferent or stale.

We have long recognized the impact of various therapeutic ingredients in the changes a client will likely undergo. We know that such factors as modeling, catharsis, empathic responding, intensive questioning, and constructive confrontation will lead to greater self-acceptance and even to personality transformations in a client. But what impact do these processes have on the one facilitating them? Can the clinician be an active instigator of the therapeutic process without, in turn, being affected by its ripple effects? Can the therapist be immune to the influence of prolonged exposure to human despair, conflict, and suffering? Can the professional helper resist the inevitable growth and self-awareness that come from studying another life? Can he or she remain the same after being in the presence of so many who are changing? Whether we like it or not, the decision to be a therapist is also a commitment to our own growth.

This process of change and growth works in mysterious ways. I had been working with a client who was exploring the utter predictability of her life. Even with success she felt stale, bored, restless, yet she was fearful of making an abrupt change that could take financial and emotional tolls. I squirmed a little, then a lot. I had just made plans to attend a professional conference I go to every year. I usually have a good time, meet some interesting people, and learn a few things I might try differently in my work. I heard my client elaborate further about her fear of taking risks. I felt even more like a hypocrite, berating her as I had for always taking the safe, predictable route. I did not even hear the last several minutes of the interview so caught up was I in reviewing the meticulous, controlled way I organize my life. Even my vacations. When the session ended I bolted for the phone.

A month later I returned from a snowcamping trip in the wilderness. This expedition, my alternative to a professional conference, gave me time to think about my life, its predictable routines, and several changes I might wish to initiate. My client, too, had changed during the interim—

though she had no idea how her crisis had precipitated my own. As she related her determination to challenge her habitual patterns I frequently nodded my head. I was nodding as much to myself as to her.

Overview of the Contents

When the first edition of *On Being a Therapist* appeared in 1986 it was one of the very few works that dealt with the personal dimensions of the helping professions, with how doing this kind of work affects us in profound, unexpected, sometimes delightful, sometimes frightening ways. This revised edition has been completely updated, retaining the personal dialogue with the reader that made this book so different from others but adding recent anecdotal and empirical research on the subject. Like its predecessor, this book is written for all practitioners of therapy — social workers, counselors, psychiatrists, psychologists, psychiatric nurses, family therapists, and other mental health specialists. It will be of utmost value to students of these professions who may be preparing for a career by learning helping skills without fully appreciating the personal consequences. Those who have experienced therapy as clients, or who are contemplating such a formidable adventure, will also find the premises contained herein of special interest.

Chapter One begins with a discussion of how primitive healers understand, intuitively, the reciprocal power between participants in the therapy process. A unified framework of the change process is presented as a backdrop for exploring further ideas about modeling and influencing power in Chapter Two. Essentially, all systems of therapy work because they share several elements: the powerful "presence" of a therapist/model, active placebos, being with the client, and structures for risk taking.

Chapter Three further explores the implications of the role of the therapist as a model by examining the relationship between personal and professional effectiveness. Just as professional skills help therapists improve their personal relationships, their real-life experiences are invaluable tools during sessions. This is the best fringe benefit of the field: constant exposure to change provides continued stimulation to promote greater personal growth, which in turn makes us more powerful models.

Chapter Four begins a discussion of the field's special hardships, including the strains of one-way intimacy, fatigue, and personal restraint. Chapter Five covers occupational hazards that result from contacts with clients who are resistant, abusive, or acting out transference issues, while Chapter Six focuses specifically on the emotional difficulties that therapists often encounter. The symptoms, causes, and cures of boredom and burnout are discussed, leading to an exploration in Chapter Seven of difficulties clinicians bring upon themselves. Examples of common self-deceptions are counterbalanced by those attributes and skills a therapist may use to promote self-healing. Additional antidotes are mentioned in Chapter Eight, which encourages the self-application of therapeutic philosophy and skills as well as group support. Chapter Nine emphasizes the influence of creativity and risk taking in the therapeutic process and personal growth.

Acknowledgments

I gratefully acknowledge the assistance of the many professionals representing the various mental health specialties and theoretical orientations who agreed to be interviewed regarding what it means to be a therapist. While most of these clinicians and therapist educators wish to remain anonymous, their words speak loudly throughout the chapters that follow. I especially thank Gracia Alkema, Becky McGovern, and Diane Blau.

I am also grateful for the indulgence of Ellen and Cary Kottler in allowing me first the solitude to live this book and then the time to write it down.

Las Vegas, Nevada   Jeffrey A. Kottler
May 1993

the author

*J*EFFREY A. KOTTLER is professor of counseling and educational psychology at the University of Nevada, Las Vegas. He studied at Oakland University, Harvard University, Wayne State University, and the University of Stockholm, and received his Ph.D. degree from the University of Virginia. He has worked as a therapist in a variety of settings including hospitals, mental health centers, schools, clinics, universities, corporations, and private practice.

Kottler is the author or coauthor of *Pragmatic Group Leadership* (1983), *Ethical and Legal Issues in Counseling and Psychotherapy: A Comprehensive Guide* (1985, 2nd ed., with William H. Van Hoose), *The Imperfect Therapist: Learning from Failure in Therapeutic Practice* (1989, with Diane S. Blau), *Private Moments, Secret Selves: Enriching Our Time Alone* (1990), *The Compleat Therapist* (1991), *Introduction to Therapeutic Counseling* (1992, 2nd ed., with Robert W. Brown), *Compassionate Therapy: Working*

With Difficult Clients (1992), *On Being a Teacher: The Personal Dimension* (1993, with Stanley Zehm), *Teacher as Counselor* (1993, with Ellen Kottler), and *Advanced Group Leadership* (1993). He has also produced an audio program with Jossey-Bass: *The Reflective Therapist: Confronting the Personal and Professional Challenges of Helping Others* (1991).

on

being

a

therapist

REVISED
EDITION

chapter 1

CLIENT AND THERAPIST:

how each
changes
the other

Sitting in a prominent place in
my office is a small vial containing an inky mixture of
earthen ingredients. It was given to me by a Peruvian witch
doctor who believed that clients influence their therapists
just as we influence them. He felt that healers, whether in
the jungle or the cities, need protection against the evil
spirits that emanate from people who are suffering.

According to an ancient Incan legend passed on from
one generation of healers to the next, all mental and physical illnesses result from an impure soul. The mental spirit of
the healer, his or her powers of suggestion and white magic,
can purify a sick soul and restore inner control. This purifica-
tion is always undertaken at great risk—for the destructive
energy dissipating from a patient also pollutes the spirit of
the healer.

Most therapists understand that they jeopardize their
own emotional well-being when they intimately encounter
the pain of others. Rogers (1972) relates the story of his

involvement with a deeply disturbed woman. He vacillated between professional aloofness and the genuine warmth that was to be his trademark. His client became confused, irrational, and hostile, and she even followed him through his relocation from Ohio State to Chicago. As her dissatisfaction with the therapy grew, she became critical and demanding of Rogers, piercing his defenses and triggering his feelings of inadequacy. "I recognized that many of her insights were sounder than mine, and this destroyed my confidence in myself; I somehow gave up *my* self in the relationship" (Rogers, 1972, p. 57). Continuing this destructive relationship eventually led to a psychotic breakdown for the client and to the borderline of a nervous breakdown for her therapist.

I wonder now if Freud's admonishment to remain detached in the therapeutic relationship was intended less to promote the client's transference than to preserve the emotional safety of the clinician. The experience of any practitioner would attest to the emotional as well as the intellectual strains of living constantly with client's crises, confusion, and intense suffering.

Our professional effectiveness, not to mention our personal well-being, are affected by the intimate relationships that have become the trademark of our work. We live with the pressure of trying to meet our own and others' expectations. Despite our best efforts to convince ourselves of our limitations, we feel responsible for clients' lives. We experience repetition and the boredom that comes from having an assembly line of people walk through our offices. We feel inadequate for not knowing enough, for not being able to help more. And as a result of these close encounters with people in pain, our own issues are constantly touched, our old wounds reopened.

Consider the experience of therapy for both participants. Confidentiality, and therefore privacy, is an implicit part of the encounter, as is a level of intimacy that sometimes reaches, if not exceeds, that of parent and child or of husband and wife. We are privy to secrets the client is barely willing to share with himself. We know the client at his best and at his worst. And as a function of spending so many intense hours together, the client comes to know us as well. We are partners in a journey.

Influence of Personal Power in Primitive Healing

Central to all that I will say on the interaction between therapist (the generic term for *counselor, social worker, psychologist, psychiatrist, mental health worker, psychiatric nurse*) and client is a relatively unified and simplistic view of change. This framework particularly emphasizes the power and influence of the therapist's personality as a facilitator of growth. The force and spirit of who the therapist is as a human being most dramatically stimulates change. Lock a person, any person, in a room alone with Sigmund Freud, Carl Rogers, Fritz Perls, Albert Ellis, or any other formidable personality, and several hours later he will come out different. It is not what the therapist does that is important—whether she interprets, reflects, confronts, or role plays—but rather who she is. A therapist who is vibrant, inspirational, charismatic; who is sincere, loving, and nurturing; who is wise, confident, and self-disciplined will have a dramatic impact through the sheer force and power of her essence, regardless of her theoretical allegiances.

The first and foremost element of change, then, is the therapist's presence—her excitement, her enthusiasm, and the power of her personality. Rollo May (1983) speaks of presence in a different sense: the complete experiencing of the client's being—not of his symptoms or problems, but of his essence. The therapist enters the relationship with clarity, openness, and serenity and comes fully prepared to encounter a soul in torment. The client comes prepared with his own expectations for a mentor, a guru, a doctor, a friend, or a wizard.

One such charismatic healer resides in a village six hundred miles north of Lima, Peru, that is sandwiched between the driest desert on earth and the world's highest tropical mountains, at the gateway to the Amazon jungle. This village is noted throughout the world because it has evolved over thousands of years as the capital of therapeutic sorcery. No fewer than one hundred witch doctors actively practice their healing arts here. Chief among them is Don Jose, an old wizard with a weathered, bronzed face and a mouth full of broken teeth.

This "primitive" witch doctor, a descendent of Incan medicine men, has an exquisite grasp of the therapeutic principles we use every day. Although he can neither read nor write and has never traveled beyond his district, he is a master of many sophisticated psychological methodologies to promote inner healing. He capitalizes on the dynamics of cohesion, intimacy, and spectator effects of vicarious learning in his group process. He carefully selects participants for his therapy, weeding out those with a poor prognosis, just as we might turn away those clients we cannot help. He conducts a preliminary interview with each candidate to gather relevant background information and to assess the candidate's mental status. During this time he also plants the seeds for cure by exuding confidence and authority.

Rather than a tweed, vested suit, Don Jose sports a special poncho and sombrero that indicate his status and prestige. His patients travel great distances and pay large sums of money to receive a cure from him. Before the ceremony ever begins, his clientele are ready and eager to change. Clearly, Don Jose conveys to them his certainty they will see rapid improvement.

His therapy consists of a series of rituals and chants. Processes of catharsis and transference, simple hypnotic inductions, and powerful drugs to promote self-exploration are also used. Underneath all the trappings — the dramatic show of hallucinating and purging on a mountaintop — lies a solid therapeutic regimen that often leads to a cure. Whether evil demons are really being exorcised or whether an active placebo response is being elicited by a sophisticated set of rituals, there is no doubt that Don Jose and his successful colleagues are powerful human beings. They have presence. They expect their clients to get better. Their clients have faith in their powers to cure.

Therapist Belief and Active Placebos

The therapeutic elements of primitive helping are part of every helping system. The witch doctor, the physician, the therapist, the teacher believe that what they do will make a difference. They have faith in their powers to cure and to promote change.

After a thorough study of many different forms of healing — including osteopathy, homeopathy, chiropractic, traditional Western medicine, acupuncture, sorcery, and psychotherapy — Andrew Weil (1983) concluded that "active placebos" most consistently account for positive results. Even the most intrusive surgical procedures work on many levels other than the obvious. In a then-classic study of a miracle cure for angina, surgeons once claimed they could reduce the pain and discomfort of inefficient arterial flow by cracking open the chest and tying off the delinquent blood vessels. Afterward, the patients experienced a dramatic cure. The inescapable conclusion: the doctors' surgical intervention saved the patient.

In a later study, patients with the same symptoms were anesthetized and operated on, but their arteries were not closed off. Nevertheless, the patients still improved! Weil believes it is the physician's or healer's expectations for a cure, coupled with some active agent (pharmaceutical, physical, psychological), that permit the body and mind to heal themselves. In the context of therapy both Frank (1961) and Fish (1973) postulate that most effective systems are designed to maximize the client's expectations for a successful outcome.

The active placebo is set in motion by the dress, setting, manner, and style of the helper and her environment. In our society, diplomas, books, leather chairs, and tweed jackets all feed into the client's expectations concerning a good therapist. And the therapeutic relationship contains within it certain nonspecific factors other than those deliberately intended by the clinician that influence a client. These placebo effects are impossible to filter out of the process. When the client experiences immediate relief after presenting complaints and initial fears in the first session, both client and therapist begin to feel optimistic.

The specifics of what the therapist does next — whether encouraging catharsis, self-control, or self-confrontation; whether using interventions of interpretation, reflection, or goal setting; whether focusing on thoughts, feelings, or behavior — probably elicit less client insight and action than does the therapist's belief that they will. The client has faith in us, as people of integrity and wisdom, as experts with the power to heal.

Techniques get in the way of good therapy when they are used as a shield to avoid intimacy with a client. "The more insecure a therapist, the more likely it is that he or she will hide behind technique, dogmatically pursuing it without it necessarily being in the best interests of the client" (Gilbert, Hughes, & Dryden, 1989, p. 8). In an even more passionate statement on this issue, Kellerman (1992), under the guise of his fictional hero Dr. Alex Delaware, remarks on the mystery and majesty of what takes place in this elusive relationship we call psychotherapy: "Sometimes they'll get better and you won't know why. Before you've even started doing what you think is so goddamn clever and hotshot scientific. Don't fight it. Just put it down to magic. It's as good an explanation as any" (p. 65).

In the absence of certainty about what is best, in the presence of someone who is needy and vulnerable, there is a compelling urge to *do* something. It has become the zeitgeist of our times to embrace technical eclecticism, prescriptive treatments, strategic interventions, behavioral management, and other forms of helping that emphasize technique. In many ways, we have permission to adapt our style and methods according to the client's needs and clinical situation. Lost in the rush toward technical innovation are the human dimensions of the relationship between people.

Despite our best efforts to research the phenomenon of the therapeutic relationship, to isolate operative ingredients, the fact remains that something magical and wonderful takes place when we create a certain kind of alliance with clients. This healing force is not unique to our profession; doctors, teachers, lawyers, even hairdressers, taxi drivers, and bartenders, offer some degree of comfort and aid in their relationships with clients—apart from the contracted services they provide. This healing relationship between people goes beyond mere catharsis: human beings have an intense craving, often unfulfilled, to be understood by someone else.

Michael Mahoney, noted primarily for his contributions as a researcher on therapeutic technique and behaviorism, is deeply moved by the personal connections of his relationships with clients. He claims that it is the privilege of witnessing another human being struggling to survive and develop that has sustained him in his work (Mahoney & Eiseman, 1989).

Mahoney does not deny that techniques provide important means of communications in therapy, in whatever theoretical language they are translated into. However, the complexity of human change requires us to acknowledge that deeper forces are at work, processes within each client that are perhaps ignited by connections with the therapist. As one client reported: "You never gave up on me. I know I am a handful. We tried so many things. The pills didn't work. Dreams were fun, but I was more interested in our dialogue about them than in their actual interpretations. I did the things we agreed I would do. I learned to talk to myself differently, like you showed me. I don't mean to sound ungrateful. Those things were certainly helpful, too. But it was our talks together that kept me going. They gave me faith. You believed in me, so I began to believe in myself. You trusted me; I learned to trust you, then myself."

Every reader will have formed an impression, perhaps even a full-fledged theory, about the change processes operating in this client's story. Some will point to the interpersonal influence, the core conditions of empathy, or the larger context of the therapeutic alliance. Others will note the cognitive interventions and the systematic homework that was completed. Still others will have been most impressed by the cathartic process, affective experiencing, consciousness raising, placebo and faith inspiration effects, or modeling processes. But what this all comes down to, what all these curative elements are reduced to, are a few factors that are operative in virtually all theoretical approaches: the force and power of the clinician's personality, the relationship between participants, and a structure to help clients think, feel, and behave differently (Kottler, 1991).

It is the last element that is the product of the previous ones. If we have been able to build a constructive alliance, if we have earned clients' respect and trust such that they are open to being influenced by us, they will venture forth and take the risks necessary to improve their lives.

Client Risk Taking in the Change Process

Much of what a therapist does is designed to motivate greater risk taking in clients. When attention is given to unresolved issues of the past, resistance and apprehensions often must be worked through. To dismantle rigid defenses, to interpret unconscious motives, to reflect on unexplored feelings may involve pushing the client to the brink of her madness. She must confront parts of herself that have been deeply buried, and she must risk the consequences of relinquishing coping strategies that have worked fairly well until this point. There is a risk, or perhaps even a certainty, that some destabilization will occur. In order for real growth to be attained, the client must be willing to experience intense confusion, disorientation, and discomfort. She leaves behind an obsolete image of herself, one that was once comfortable and familiar, and she risks not liking the person she will become. She will lose a part of herself that can never be recovered. She risks all this for the possibility of a better existence, and all she has to go on is the therapist's word.

When the client seeks to modify specific goals and behaviors, the risks are even more evident. To change any single aspect of one's behavior is to set in motion a chain reaction of subsequent aftershocks. One woman had been procrastinating for years in therapy, reluctant to take any action. As is usually the case, all her difficulties were connected—her dead-end job, her desire to move away from her parents, her relationships with men, and her desire to lose weight. If she were to make a change in any one of these areas, she would risk having everything else tumble down. The idea of losing even fifteen pounds was frightening to her since it would mean she would be more attractive, feel more confident, have demonstrated the capacity for self-control, and have proven the power to change. She just could not face the consequences of changing any part of her life since that would mean every other part would have to change as well. It was much easier to come to therapy each week and please her therapist with good intentions, a cooperative attitude, and a wonderful capacity for generating insights that would not necessarily lead to change.

The therapist's job is to do everything in her power not just to promote self-understanding but to encourage risk taking. The client must not only reflect but act. This task is accomplished not only by the quality of one's interventions, designed to reduce the perceived threat and increase the willingness to experiment, but by the genuine commitment the therapist makes to risk taking in her own life. A professional who believes in the value of risk taking is one who has varied experiences in taking calculated chances when the need arises. This courage, as it is modeled in the sessions, begets courage in the clients.

Risks of the Therapist

There are tremendous risks for the therapist in living with the anguish of others, in being so close to others' torments. Sometimes we become desensitized by human emotion and experience an acute overdose of feeling; we turn ourselves off. At other times we overreact to personal incidents as a result of lingering dissonance created during sessions.

I was cross-country skiing in the woods with my wife. The sun was blazing, reflecting off the snow. We were breathing hard, enjoying the scenery and the synchronized movement of our bodies. Quite suddenly, without any warning, I abruptly stopped in my tracks and started crying. Needless to say, my wife was a little surprised.

She asked me what was wrong, especially since a few moments earlier I had been feeling such joy. I finally blurted out the question: "Are you going to leave me?" She looked at me as if I were a raving lunatic and replied "Of course not!" She reassured me with a hug and tried to find out what was going on. I explained that lately in my practice a number of female clients had been working on issues of freedom and independence. They felt trapped in their marriages and resented their husbands' needs for approval and dominance. After years of struggle with and resistance from their husbands, they had chosen divorce as the only solution for liberation. Again and again I heard their words ringing in my ears: "Why is he so oblivious to what I want and what I feel? He thinks things are so great between us just because he finds me home at night. When he finally realizes how serious I am about making changes it will be too late. He has no idea how bad things are, and he doesn't want to know."

For weeks the effect of hearing these words in several different keys had been accumulating, and it had begun eating away at my own illusions of security. Was I, like the husbands of my clients, on the verge of divorce while blissfully denying my problems—while enjoying an afternoon in the woods? Fortunately, my concern was unnecessary, but I felt shell-shocked from the close proximity to other people's battlefields.

Physicians take careful steps to protect themselves from the infection, disease, and suffering of their patients. Rubber gloves, surgical masks, and probing stainless steel instruments keep germs at arm's length. But sometimes there is a seepage of pain. For one practicing physician (Moss, 1981), all barriers between himself and his patients eroded because he let himself feel too much when his hands were exploring inside their visceral organs.

Throughout the process of therapy, being with the client is our main instrument of cure. Although we try to insulate ourselves, and we successfully pretend most of the time, leaks inevitably occur. As our nonpossessive warmth, caring, and power radiate toward the client, stimulating change, so, too, do we experience intimacy, dependence, discomfort, and transference and countertransference reactions that permanently alter our perceptions and internal structure.

To take on a client, any client, is to make a tremendous commitment to that person that could last years if not a lifetime. For better or worse, no matter how the client behaves, the therapist feels an obligation to be available, understanding, and compassionate. From the moment a client settles himself in the chair for the first time, we take a deep breath knowing that what is about to occur is the beginning of a new relationship. It will have moments of special closeness and others of great hardship. The client will, at times, worship the therapist, scorn him, abuse him, ignore him, play with him, and want to devour him. And through it all, regardless of what is going on in his own life — sickness, births, deaths, joys, disappointments — the therapist must be there for the client, always waiting.

If we ever really considered the possible risks in getting involved with a client, we would not do so for any price. Never mind that we will catch their colds and flus — what about their pessimism, negativity, and psychopathology? One just cannot see clients week after week, listen to their stories, and dry their tears without being profoundly affected by the experience. There are risks for the therapist he will not recognize until years later. Images stay with us until the grave. Words creep back to haunt us. Those silent screams remain deafening.

Therapist Vulnerability

Watching a therapist enter his office with nothing but a briefcase, one would never imagine that he is preparing to enter into mortal combat. Things appear quite civilized and controlled on the surface, what with the polite greetings and all. But once the action starts, the sparks that fly may leave third-degree burns. In a small room there is nowhere to seek shelter. The therapist uses only his naked self (figuratively, of course) as the instrument of treatment, a condition that requires tremendous self-control and exacts considerable vulnerability. To meet the client in a therapeutic encounter we must leave behind our armor and defenses. We must go out from our centeredness as far as we dare. In our effort to be open and receptive, to participate with the client in the relationship, to venture forth as far as we are able, we risk losing our own identity (May, 1983).

Great wracking sobs could be heard through the door, not an unusual occurrence in a psychiatric clinic except that the client had left five minutes earlier. Only the therapist remained — alone, behind the closed door. Tears streamed down his face. He was huddled in a ball on the floor. The therapist had been conducting a particularly intense session with a man who was mourning the loss of his unborn son. As he was helping the client accept the miscarriage and find hope in the future, he realized at some point that he was no longer speaking to the client but to himself. His own girlfriend had decided unceremoniously, upon ending their relationship, to abort their baby. The therapist had long ago worked through his loss, pain, and disappointment. Yet it all came tumbling forth again as his client struggled with a similar issue. Against all restraint, all objectivity, all desire to help the client, he lost the separateness between himself and the other.

It would be senseless to complain about the side effects that stem from personal involvement. After all, many of us entered this profession in the first place because of an interest in resolving our own issues along the path of helping others. I am embarrassed to admit that although I did and do feel a commitment toward altruism, a significant part of my motivation to become a therapist came from my needs to make sense of the world, to stave off my fear of mediocrity, to find acceptance, to satisfy my desire for control, to win approval and gratitude. I ask myself why I care so much about writing these words, why I continue to write books, and I laugh at the pat yet incomplete response: because I have something to say that others might find useful. But that is not the whole truth. I also desperately want to be liked and thrive on external validation.

When a client comes in and struggles with these very themes (since I am looking for them, I see them everywhere), I rejoice in the opportunity to do some more work on myself. There are times, however, when I lose perspective and become so intertwined in the relationship that I must take a few steps out of range in order to untangle my own vulnerabilities from those of my client.

The therapist is vulnerable not only to the loss of self but also to annihilation through assaults on her self-esteem.

We may profess to be neutral and to have no vested interest in the outcome, but we care quite a bit about how things turn out. It is impossible to care deeply for people without caring about what they do. When clients do not improve or get worse, we not only feel their pain but take it personally that they are not cooperating with our therapeutic efforts. This is in spite of our attempts to remember the golden words: "We do our part, the client must do his" or "It is ultimately up to the client to change." All of this might very well be true, but we have a lot at stake as well. We can act unconcerned when a client does not improve, shrug our shoulders and go about our business, tell ourselves we are doing all we can, then head for the beach. But others will make decisions about our competence and attack our credibility even if we do not.

The client's family members, for example, having been in the unenviable position of having to live with the client while we only see her an hour or two per week, cannot afford much patience. It is easy for us to tell them: "Give it time. This has taken a long time to develop into a problem, and it will take a while to resolve." They will thank us politely as they mutter under their breaths, "This guy doesn't know what he's doing." Then they will express their opinions to all who will listen, exasperated and exhausted. Since everyone knows a therapist he or she likes, the family's confidence will be further undermined by friends who suggest they consult Dr. X, who really knows what she is doing.

And let us not pretend that it does not hurt when a client abruptly quits treatment with the following farewell:

"Gee, I know you've tried so hard to help me. And I agree it's probably all my fault. But since I've been seeing you I've only gotten worse. You asked me to be patient and I think I have been, but it doesn't seem to help. My cousin is seeing another therapist, Dr. X. Perhaps you know her? Well, anyway, I'm going to be switching to her. Thanks for all you've done." Now, not only will Dr. X find out how ineffective we have been (because she is surely not going to assume the lack of progress was the client's fault), but soon the referral source will call wanting to know how things are going. We can make up some excuse about "primitive defenses" or "resistance" that we may even believe, and maybe the referral source will buy it, but deep, deep inside is a quiet little voice that will say: "You blew it." If such an episode occurs in the same week in which we have a few too many cancellations, we are well on our way to a major bout of self-doubt.

Pressure to Perform

Therapy is a performance profession. We are judged by our peers based on our ability to produce results. We must, then, contend with the risks of putting our reputations on the line with every case we take on. We may be forgiven for an occasional lapse, or a client who is particularly stubborn, but we nevertheless feel an assault on our personal as well as our professional competence when we believe we have failed a client.

Some practitioners encounter no such self-doubts. Perhaps they are part of a system that allows them to pass the primary responsibility for results along to the client. They believe that it is their job to be there for the client, to listen, and to interpret or reflect when required. But it is up to the client to change when she is good and ready.

Haley (1984), de Shazer (1988), and O'Hanlon and Weiner-Davis (1989) have attempted to change this conception of the therapist's role by placing more emphasis on an active, directive posture. They view the idea of resistance as a figment of the therapist's imagination designed to avoid responsibility for a cure. In strategic approaches such as Haley's there are even more risks at stake—risks for both client and therapist. When the clinician attempts to intervene actively, there is a greater likelihood that the client will be either helped or harmed. The techniques and directives tend to be dramatic and are designed to be intrusive. When they work, they work instantly. When they do not work, some people get very angry.

The therapist takes risks with some of her most powerful interventions—those that produce the most dramatic results. Virginia Satir, for example, in working with conflicted families, made herself extremely vulnerable and risked rejection by shaming herself in front of her clients. She also tested the trust level in her alliance by disclosing feelings the client might not have been ready to hear: "I want to say something, and Coby,...I'm taking a big risk at this moment...I feel, and I've been feeling this for about the last ten minutes, that I want to take you in my arms. Not because you're a baby, but because I think in your insides you've had all this longing to have something" (Satir & Baldwin, 1983, p. 92).

Confrontation takes a heavy toll on the therapist as well as on the client. There is no greater feeling of victory for a clinician than in the moments just after a client has responded to confrontation that is well timed and well received. Yet when confrontation falls flat or ignites defensive anger, the clinician may feel thoroughly frustrated. Although the client's safety must be kept firmly in mind, there is no place for meekness and excessively conservative intervention in the therapeutic encounter. We are paid specifically to say things to the client that nobody else has the courage and finesse to say. By giving the client honest feedback regarding his behavior, we take the risk that he will be unwilling or unable to deal with the reality of his situation. By withholding crucial clinical assessments that the client has a perfect right to hear, we waste his time and money because of our own fears of making a mistake. The therapist is thus saddled with the responsibility of judging just when calculated risks may be taken, when the client can best handle the painful truth. An error in judgment could result in a tragedy or at least in regressive backlash.

One of the most difficult dilemmas is encountered when we believe a client is a danger to himself and/or others. Of course, there are guidelines to follow, but they are sometimes designed more to protect the therapist from litigation than to help the client. If we have evidence that the client has any serious homicidal or suicidal intent, we are obligated to follow through with commitment proceedings.

If we are hesitant and postpone such action to give the client some time to straighten out, we risk tremendous liability should the client attempt to take his life or that of someone else. And if we protect ourselves and society from the threat of harm, we may do so at the expense of the client, who will be subjected to numerous indignities.

Therapy is an exercise in risk taking for both participants. If we are not hypocrites, then we are models of change-in-action for our clients. We demonstrate our effectiveness through the force of our personalities and through our willingness to be with the client in a loving and respectful way. We believe in ourselves and in our clients. The elements of change in any theoretical approach converge in the very personal style of every practitioner. To be genuine, to truly accompany a client during his journey of self-exploration requires selfless devotion during forty-five-minute intervals. We eventually feel the wear and tear of such devotion, or, alternately, we experience complete detachment from the world and from the feelings behind our professional stance.

STRUGGLES FOR
POWER AND INFLUENCE

$\mathcal{A}$s we are all well aware, growth occurs spontaneously without professional help. Many theories offer explanations of this phenomenon. Psychological growth may be part of our genetically programmed survival instinct or may be reinforced by the environment and society. There are developmental, phenomenological, sociobiological, behavioral, and countless other explanations for spontaneous, unstructured change processes. To complicate matters further, the interpersonal influence that operates in therapy moves in both directions. Just as the therapist attempts to do everything in his power to change clients, so, too, do clients seek to control the therapist for their own purposes (Strong, 1982).

Thus, a two-way interchange of social influence exists between client and therapist, and they have a reciprocal modeling effect on one another (Dorn, 1984). The therapist intentionally and spontaneously mobilizes whatever personal power she has available to intensify modeling processes as these work to influence the client to change. At the same time, the client, reacting to the seductive influences of this personal power, is deliberately and unconsciously fighting for control of the sessions. The client attempts to act out the transference and mold the therapist into someone else. He will also model ways of expressing himself that the therapist will begin to parrot. If the two people locked together in this combat of interpersonal influence spend enough time together, one of them will begin to reach his or her desired goals, while both of them will change in ways that neither could ever have anticipated.

Spontaneous Modeling

As the Socratic era of teaching by personal example, Freud's proposal of identification processes, and Bandura's reworking of social learning theory have shown, people are strongly influenced by exposure to other, more powerful people. Thus, one main force of childhood is the overpowering urge to grow up and be just like mommy or daddy, sister, Wonder Woman, Superman, teacher, or the kid down the block. Even in adulthood, models in the media continue to exert a powerful influence on people's behavior. Whenever people go to a sporting event or movie, turn on the radio or television set, or open a newspaper or magazine, they begin to adopt the values attributed to the image of a celebrity (Caughey, 1978).

Even after we learn to stop idolizing our heroes and parents and to prize new values of independence and self-sufficiency, models continue to exert a powerful influence on the way we dress, speak, feel, and think. In fact, the mentor system is the core of most therapist education: teachers, advisers, supervisors, authors, and colleagues shape who we are and the way we practice our craft. For many therapists, the first decade of our professional lives is spent imitating the master clinicians before we ever consider what we really believe in our hearts.

For most people, unstructured learning is often spontaneously ignited by first exposure to a significant model. Dissonance is immediately experienced when comparisons are made between the model and the self. People feel tremendously inadequate and incompetent after they enter a relationship with someone who appears confident and in control. Yet there is the birth of hope and resolve. On some level they believe it is possible that they, too, can assimilate those qualities they most admire.

Therapists as Professional Models

In the early stages of identification, the model is idealized and made even larger than life. His power is therefore intensified, as is his influencing capability. The apprenticeship of the therapist to his mentor, not unlike the relationship between client and therapist, begins in this way and continues through the stages of worship, subservience, dependent love, work, work, more work, mutual respect, and briefly, equality, before the final loss and return to self-direction.

Models give lots of reinforcement to those who express an interest in being just like them. Narcissism pervades our domain. Therapists, teachers, and other professional models such as actors and athletes thrive on gratitude and accolades from fans and disciples. The only difference is that public figures receive financial compensation equal to their aura. Therapists are limited to the ceiling established by their hourly rates or their salaries. The balance of payment is usually received in the intangible benefits that accrue from hero worship.

It is galling to hear "crazy shrink" stories in which a therapist is portrayed in the media or in social conversations as being more disturbed than any of his or her clients. In an *Atlantic Monthly* article about how emotionally unstable, narcissistic, and "wounded" many therapists are, one woman is quoted by Maeder (1989) as saying that every time she goes to a party, invariably the most foolish, embarrassing, and crazy person in attendance is a therapist. As further evidence for his arguments, Maeder (p. 37) quotes a president of the American Academy of Psychotherapists addressing the members of his own organization: "When I first visited a national psychiatric convention, in 1943, I was dismayed to find the greatest collection of oddballs, Christ beards, and psychotics that I had ever seen outside a hospital."

We perpetuate the myth of our own personal ineptitude. Some readers (social workers, counselors, psychologists, family therapists) probably nodded to themselves as they read the preceding passage, saying to themselves,

"Yeah, psychiatrists *are* crazy," just as they might say the same thing about colleagues in other professions. It just burns me, though, when I encounter a professional who asks clients to do things that he or she cannot do. What kind of image do we project to the public when we cannot demonstrate in our own lives the most rudimentary degree of empathy, sincerity, and emotional stability?

In the classroom and in business the mentor or modeling system has been operating for centuries. In the process of therapy interpersonal influencing power has developed unprecedented effectiveness. Since we are good at managing conflicts, coping with transitions, and heading off predictable crises, the intense trauma associated with "termination" has been substantially reduced. Rarely do clients part company with their therapists seeing them as enemies to be debunked.

Many of the joys as well as the hazards of our field result from the consequences of being professional models. We want to show our clients, by the way we live our lives, that it is possible to be happy and that this desire serves as a powerful incentive to be fulfilled human beings. Clients know nothing about the details of our existence, our dreams, our disappointments, or what we are like in social situations, yet they know our spirit intimately. They can sense our moods, feel our tranquility, confidence, and energy. They may not know what we are really like, but they know us at our absolute best. We do not impatiently yell at our clients as we might our own children. We try not to meet our own needs at all during sessions. And clients come to love us, to worship our idealized self. Even though we understand the illusions and myths we may be creating, we still have a wonderful opportunity to be more like clients think we actually are — completely loving, giving, peaceful, and in control.

Balancing Omnipotence and Humanness

The therapist has become the contemporary equivalent of the oracle perched on a mountaintop; clients are the pilgrims who journey in search of enlightenment (Kopp, 1972). Mistrusting their own inner voices and lacking self-direction, clients look to their gurus for guidance and see them as embodiments of power.

The principal hazard of our profession is the narcissistic belief that we really are special (Herron & Rouslin, 1984; Welt & Herron, 1990). The therapist's office is an unreal world in which distractions are minimized and rituals are carefully observed. The therapist controls most of the show. Although the client chooses the content, the therapist directs the script and the interpretation of the lines.

Most therapists do good work. Clients get better. They feel grateful and ascribe their improvement to something or someone outside of themselves. We are more than willing to take partial credit; it is good for new referrals and our sense of potency. The problem is not in feeling that we have made some difference in a client's life but in forgetting that we are not the paragons we would like to be. When we direct the interacting, questioning, controlling, confronting, nurturing, and even summarizing at appropriate intervals for eight hours a day, it is an abrupt shock to our systems to find ourselves at home or with friends struggling to be heard like everyone else.

We are used to being listened to. Some people even take notes on what we say, and we can test them later to make sure they were paying attention. After a while we start believing that we are important. Clients and students reinforce the idea by telling us how much they were helped. Then we remember how fragile the illusion of omnipotence really is. Even if it is initially useful for clients to idealize their therapists, we help them and ourselves to see a separate reality.

Modeling takes the form of presenting not only an ideal to strive for, but a real, live person who is flawed, genuine, and sincere. Occasionally, self-disclosure can be used judiciously to close the psychological distance between therapist and client, to increase the perceived similarity. Many clients are greatly relieved to learn that their therapists have been the victims of the same self-defeating behaviors they are now trying to overcome. By revealing a model of humanness, with accompanying imperfections, the therapist can help the client feel less overwhelmed and more optimistic that relative personal mastery is indeed within reach. The therapist thus walks a fine line between exuding a certain assurance and personal competence and coping with her unique eccentricities. She must battle with the consequences of acting like an impromptu guru much of the day and then successfully make the transition to flawed normalcy during the rest of her time.

Mentor's Strength of Character

Most of the great teachers we have ever known or heard of were charismatic individuals. Plato, Socrates, Confucius, Freud, and Marx were geniuses in mastering their fields' knowledge, but their true talent was in imparting their wisdom and recruiting disciples through the force of their personalities. Contemporary media teachers such as physicist Carl Sagan, biologist Lewis Thomas, and sex educator Ruth Westheimer demonstrate the power of attractive personalities in promoting learning. Their followers are as much seduced by their voices, smiles, humor, and presence as they are fascinated by what they say.

The leaders in the field of psychotherapy have made many significant contributions from their research and ideas. However, nobody would have listened to Freud, Jung, Rogers, Frankl, Ellis, Perls, or Adler if they had not been captivating people. Their unique ways of expressing themselves, their passion and excitement, their energy and spirit, their commitment and confidence gave life to their ideas. It was their eccentric quirks, their personal struggles, their humanity that were so attractive.

Peck (1978, p. 122) tells of his mystical experience in listening to a mentor lecture on a subject that was mostly incomprehensible. He concentrated on the speech with an intensity in which "sweat was literally dripping down my face. . . . I was willing to do this. . . because I recognized his greatness and that what he had to say would likely be of great value." Fine (1972, pp. 224–225) also recalls a memorable lecture: "What he said I do not know, but I do remember his flashing eyes and the forcefulness of his personality."

Good therapists have a way of communicating similar greatness — of making the listener feel that what they have to say is worth listening to no matter how much effort is required to hear. They accomplish this through the intrinsic appeal of their inner voices. The radical psychoanalyst Jacques Lacan was purposely obtuse: "If they knew what I was saying. . . they would never let me say it" (quoted in Schneiderman, 1983, p. 11). And his behavior was completely outrageous: "Once at Vincennes he told a group of revolutionary students that he could not be expected to have an intelligent dialogue with them because they didn't even know what aphasia was. The students were incensed, and one protested on the spot by taking his clothes off. Lacan responded that he had seen better the night before" (p. 29). Yet these factors only added to his appeal. It was Lacan's eccentricities, his controversies as much as his theories, that attracted so much attention.

All effective therapists intuitively find a way to capitalize on the strengths of their characters. Freud's self-analytic skills, Rogers's genuineness, Ellis's capacity for rational thinking, Whitaker's playfulness, formed the nucleus for their respective theories. So, too, do clinicians translate their inner selves into a personal style of helping.

The Ideal Therapist Model

Even with all our differences in values, interests, histories, and training, most therapists share similar attributes as powerful helping models. Many researchers, theoreticians, and practitioners have attempted to describe or even to quantify the dimensions of a therapeutic personality (Beutler, 1983; Corey, Corey, & Callanan, 1988; Decker, 1988; Kottler, 1991). Rogers mentioned qualities such as genuineness, openness, and acceptance. Carkhuff specified empathic understanding and the ability to respond. Jerome Frank felt confidence was the key to a therapist's persuasive power. Maslow believed the more general striving for self-actualization was a crucial trait.

Whether through a deliberate and systematic indoctrination in certain beliefs ("Life is not fair" or "Confrontation is better than avoidance") or as a by-product of interpersonal intimacy, clients come to know our basic values about life, no matter how much we try to disguise them. Some practitioners deny that this is so, claiming that perfect neutrality and complete objectivity are possible. Perhaps those who practice within a strict psychoanalytic framework are indeed able to withhold most of their values from their clients. However, as a veteran participant in psychoanalytic therapy many years ago, I can attest that although my therapist tried to keep herself out of the sessions, I knew exactly what she wanted me to say and do and the choices she preferred that I make. Being an expert approval seeker from way back when, I worked very hard to be as much like her as I possibly could — including entering her profession so that I might embrace even more of her values.

If this assumption is true, that clients take on our values as a consequence (deliberate or incidental) of participation in treatment, we had better be sure that what we espouse is well grounded in reality and generally healthy. The ideal therapist is comfortable with herself and appears warm, tolerant, sincere, serene, tranquil, and self-assured. This quiet confidence is counterbalanced by a contagious zest for life. Passion. Excitement. Electricity. Enthusiasm. She radiates from body and soul.

We have the client's attention. He is attracted to compassion and a loving nature. Offering much more than the wooden skills and platitudes of "advanced accurate level empathy," "unconditional positive regard," and other "primary facilitative factors," the therapist genuinely cares about the client's welfare. These feelings go beyond restrained professional respect for someone who trusts us. The client can feel our caring, our intense desire to give of ourselves.

But love is not enough. If it were, parents could heal their children with intention alone. The therapist is a person of wisdom and knowledge. She is an expert in human nature. She is perceptive and sensitive. She is a student of science and the arts, of the abstract and ambiguous, and especially of language. She hears. She sees, smells, touches, and feels with great accuracy.

The therapist is also attractive for her stability and grounding. She is patient, so, so patient. She exhibits great self-discipline, yet, enigmatically, she is also spontaneous and playful. Creativity, humor, flexibility, honesty, and sincerity are other qualities to strive for.

Our main job is to make ourselves as attractive and

powerful as possible in order to lend greater potency to our interventions. We communicate on two levels simultaneously. First, there is the content of what we say: the accuracy of our interpretations, the truth of our confrontations, and the appropriateness of our metaphors make a difference in client awareness, insight, and behavior. On a more subtle, preconscious level, the client also attends to our style. Much of our interpersonal influence, our power as models, operates in the nonverbal realm. It is the way we speak as much as what we say that communicates confidence and favorable expectations. It is the way we carry ourselves that implies genuineness and sincerity in our movements.

We try to teach goodness, honesty, and trustworthiness in our sessions. Such qualities cannot be faked. That is not to say that deceitful therapists are never effective, because some are. But to the degree that we can make our spirit and energy purer, we enable our words to carry even more power. As professional helpers, then, our primary task is to be more personally effective and loving human beings. We should show compassion not only in our work but in our lives as well. If we are to be consistent and genuine, then our family, colleagues, friends, and even strangers on the street deserve the best of us as well.

I have always found it ironic that clients who pay for my time, people whom I would rarely choose as friends, receive 95 percent of my attention, my focused concentration. The people I truly love the most get me in diluted form, distracted and self-involved. As I am writing these words my son calls my name. I put him off: "Be with you in a minute.

Let me finish what I'm doing." I would never do that with a client whose ramblings were interrupting an important thought. I give my best to people who pay for my time. Must my son make an appointment and pay me to get my undivided attention?

How Modeling Works in Therapy

Bandura (1977) and other researchers have described the uses of modeling in specific, behaviorally defined situations. These social learning theorists are fond of investigating those factors that enhance the acquisition of learning, the quality of performance, and the transfer and generalization of behavior (Perry & Furukawa, 1980). For our purposes, however, we are less concerned with the details of vicarious reinforcement processes than with the broader understanding of the different ways modeling operates in therapy.

For example, on the most ambiguous and elusive level, the therapist's energy has a significant impact on the client's mood and conduct. Therapists who sit peacefully, sagely, speaking in silky and serene tones seem to tranquilize even the most agitated clients. Anxious, high-strung people, those with fears, phobias, and panic disorders, respond well to calm models. They learn from our manner of interaction, the way we sit and stand, the pace of our speaking and listening just how a relaxed person functions. On the other hand, when a therapist's energy is animated, electric, vibrating throughout the room, even the most passive people will wake up a bit. Clients respond to the personal energy we generate. They admire our intense vibrancy and the self-control to modulate it. As models, we remain living examples of constructive human energy.

Clients deliberately and sometimes unconsciously adopt their therapists' speech patterns, favorite expressions, even mannerisms and dress habits. Groups of graduate students can be identified with their advisers with only brief verbalizations as cues. After decades we can still trace remnants in our vocabularies to the influences of significant mentors. With that kind of imitative learning occurring without deliberate encouragement, it is incredible to consider the potential power of strategic therapeutic modeling.

The simplest form of modeling occurs during those instances when the therapist spontaneously demonstrates desirable behaviors. During a typical session, regardless of the content, a client may receive instruction in effective confrontation, appropriate questioning, or comfortably handling silence. Attention may be drawn to the therapist's assertive posture, internally based language, concise statements, or creative thinking.

The use of simulated experiences in therapy provides even more specific imitative learning. Psychodramatic and other rehearsal or role-played structures usually contain a segment that is demonstrated by the therapist. A restrained and timid client who is practicing a confrontation with a family member will be asked during periods of frustration to observe the expert model in action. The therapist will then show a variety of ways to defuse conflict and maintain control.

Therapists have been known to employ a number of interventions that have modeling principles at their core: (1) rehearsing role-playing that emphasizes recurrent themes, (2) showing videotapes that demonstrate desired target behaviors, (3) teaching discrimination skills through observing models, (4) reviewing taped segments of oneself engaged in new behaviors, (5) using puppets in play therapy, (6) using anecdotes or stories to illustrate principles, (7) embedding metaphors in communication to model effective behavior vicariously without the client's feeling threatened, and (8) using language carefully to demonstrate self-responsibility. In modeling acceptance and a caring attitude toward clients, we hope that they will internalize these qualities to neutralize their self-critical natures. Via demonstration we are also introducing them to a set of beliefs and values that will prove more constructive in resolving their difficulties (Decker, 1988).

Metaphoric anecdotes can range from fairy tales to more personal self-disclosures that minimize the psychological distance between therapist and client. By modeling openness, strength, even vulnerability and the sharing of intense feelings, the therapist invites the client to follow the lead. Trust, perceived similarity, and empathic understanding can be vastly improved through restrained, well-timed, and appropriate therapist sharing that is devoid of self-indulgence. Reviewing the literature related to the power of a therapist's interpersonal influence, McConnaughy (1987) concluded that clinicians who are perceived as trustworthy, attractive, and personally credible are more persuasive in their work.

The Uses of Power

Modeling strategies also share a belief in the benevolent and judicious use of power. A clinician's power is first sanctioned by legitimate bodies such as licensing boards. The diplomas on our walls are perceived to endow us with certain mystical powers to read minds. As such, we are viewed not only as legitimate professionals endowed with special privileges but as figures of authority. Depending on the client's previous experiences with other models of authority (school principal, safety patrol, drill sergeant, parents, and teachers), the therapist's power also can instill feelings of resentment and rebellion.

Power is what infuses us with the persuasion and influence to motivate clients to change. When used in the spiritual rather than a manipulative sense—that is, for the client's self-articulated good rather than to meet our own needs—power is the driving force behind everything we do. It gives weight to what we say and commands sufficient attention that clients will allow themselves to be influenced by our messages. Eventually, there is a gradual transfer of power in which clients take on the roles and responsibilities that we have modeled. They have internalized the best parts of us.

If we accept our responsibility as therapist-models and agree to use our influence for the good of our clients, we are then committed to increasing our personal and professional effectiveness. We are involved in the process of integrating our various roles and making ourselves as appealing and as influential as we are capable of becoming.

chapter *3*

PERSONAL AND
PROFESSIONAL LIVES

*t*he practice of psychotherapy permits a unique life-style in which one's personal and professional roles complement each other. There are few other careers in which the boundaries between work and play are so permeable. All the powers of observation, perception, sensitivity, and diagnosis are equally useful with clients, family, or friends. The skills we use in our work, such as empathic listening or flexible problem solving, prove invaluable when helping the people we love. In a similar vein, all our personal experiences, our travels, learnings, conversations, readings, and intimate dealings with life's joys and sorrows, provide the foundation for everything we do in our therapy sessions.

Spurling and Dryden (1989) discuss the practice of therapy as a calling. It is their observation that the master clinicians they studied all feel driven to understand the human condition. They have an insatiable curiosity about and need to make sense of their life experiences and to help others to do so. This process moves in the opposite direction as well: by helping people to put their lives in perspective, to unlock the hidden secrets of their psyches, to know themselves more thoroughly, we are helping ourselves to do the same. We are searching for answers to life's ultimate questions. Finding others who will help subsidize this quest (or an agency that will offer financial support) only makes this journey less lonely and more comfortable. Searching for truth in the tradition of Lao-tzu, Buddha, or Confucius is admirable, but it is a lot more fun when we do not have to do so as paupers.

This emotional and intellectual hunger that drives many therapists has its dangers as well. "For such people their jobs are not merely a way to earn a living: it is the essence of their lives" (Maeder, 1989, p. 37). Personal and professional roles become fused when the therapist is always "on duty" and thus unable or unwilling to have a life outside of work and beyond the role of helper.

Fusion of Roles

In their research on practicing therapists, Henry, Sims, and Spray (1973) discovered that most adopt a unidimensional attitude toward all their relationships, whether they be with clients, friends, or family. There is a "distancing aura" in which the clinician detaches himself not only from the therapeutic encounter but also from the activities of professional societies and home life. There is also remarkable consistency in the way clients change in sessions and in the way therapists made their decisions to enter the field. Most practitioners were more strongly influenced by personal considerations such as cultural heritage or rejection of parental values than by any professional models. In most therapists there seems to be a burning desire to work through personal conflicts, a conviction that helping solve others' problems can help one solve his or her own problems, and a tendency to merge the personal and professional dimensions of life into a unified perception of self and world.

The fusion of personal and professional dimensions in a therapist's life affects not only her life-style, emotional stability, and values but also the course her sessions take. It is naive to pretend that the client assumes complete responsibility for introducing the content and direction of treatment. We may start with what he believes is his problem, but in no time we take over to lead discussions toward the topic we think is most important—whether it be feelings toward parents, underlying thought patterns, or specific behaviors at work. Furthermore, except for the most conservative practitioners who follow the tenets of their theory to the letter, there is a certain amount of inconsistency and unreliability in our helping efforts, depending on what our mood is at the time, what is currently going on in our lives, what we have recently finished doing or thinking about, and what we are planning to do next.

It is no extraordinary revelation to admit that events in our lives affect the outcome of our work. Why, then, do we act as though therapy is simply the application of scientifically tested principles and reliable therapeutic interventions to the specific circumstances of a client's life? We act as though the process is always the same; as though there is always a progression through identical stages, resolution of oedipal and transference conflicts, disputing of the same irrational beliefs; as though the therapist is always a constant. Many of the leading therapists believe that reliability in helping methodologies is the most important issue in the field.

Regardless of what we may wish to believe, the practice of therapy is a distinctly human enterprise that is significantly affected by myriad random and personal variables. Although it is laudable to work toward greater consistency in the way we treat clients, a therapist is a fallible human being subject to quirks, biases, errors, misjudgments, and spectacular distortions of reality. Even with the best education, training, supervision, study, and self-analysis, a therapist is hardly the anonymous, perfectly stable, neutral, all-knowing, and accepting creator that clients prefer to see.

Consider, for example, the potential impact of various personal events on professional behavior. Bellack and Faithorn (1981) and Guy (1987) review several "intercurrent events," such as marriage, divorce, childbirth, moving, illness, and death, in a therapist's life and explore how the client's feelings and behavior are affected. Any physical change, such as a leg cast, missing wedding band, weight loss, or the like, can hardly be ignored by the client. Certainly such life transitions and crises cannot be fully shelved by the person experiencing them, even for forty-five minutes while someone else is talking. Perhaps the best evidence of how a therapist's increased vulnerability can change the nature of treatment is the observation that the majority of therapist/client sexual improprieties occur with therapists who have been recently divorced. It is also inconceivable that a therapist who has a baby growing within her, or pain radiating up his spine, or severe financial difficulties, or who has experienced the death of a loved one, is going to conduct therapy in exactly the same way as he or she would if these conditions did not exist.

Oh, You're a Therapist?

As therapists we do two kinds of helping—formal therapy within our professional domain, complete with all the trappings; and "kinda therapy," in which friends, relatives, acquaintances, even complete strangers, ask us for advice. Of course, we attempt to dispense with this advice ambush with a feeble protest: "I'm not on duty right now" or "I think it would be best if I referred you to a colleague." But the reality is that we are never really off duty. We cannot just stop using what we know and can do. Almost against our will, we find ourselves sorting out arguments or listening to people's complaints.

One new therapist, for example, struggled with the confusion surrounding her personal and professional roles. She had volunteered her time to work with AIDS patients. Once it was discovered what she did for a living, she was assigned to a family to help them work through issues related to death and dying. What was her role in this helping effort? She was not actually their therapist, more like a friend. Could she ask them personal questions, or would that be prying? Maybe she should extricate herself from the situation altogether, so confusing was her ambiguous role.

This fusion of personal and professional roles underlies some of the risks inherent in intimacy with clients. Sorting out dual relationships has become the most prevalent ethical issue of our time (Herlihy & Corey, 1992).

Risking and Intimacy

Intimacy means being open, unguarded, and close to another. To facilitate trust, the therapist must feel comfortable facing intimacy without fear. This closeness helps the client to feel understood and appreciated; it teaches him that true intimacy is indeed possible, that a relationship based on regard and respect is desirable. Through the mutual risking that takes place between the two partners in the relationship, both learn to appreciate better what closeness can bring. Through their willingness to be honest and open, committed to the betterment of the client's life, both participants experience the risk of intimacy.

Because therapeutic relationships are intensely personal and often quite intimate encounters in which participants feel a mutual attraction, there is tension and confusion associated with the way they are structured (Derlega, Hendrick, Winstead, & Berg, 1991). We know more about our clients than we know about most of our friends. We spend more time each week engaged in meaningful, deep, intimate conversation with a given client than we do with most of the other people in our lives, sometimes even more than with the people we live with. Before you deny this proposition, consider how many friends or family members you arrange to be with on a regular basis with whom you: (1) talk only about personal matters of great significance, (2) do not allow yourself to be distracted by any intrusions, and (3) confront one another when you sense the other is being evasive or less than truthful. Even with the asymmetrical, inequitable, one-sided professional dimensions of our relationships with clients, they are nevertheless moving, personal interchanges. They carry many of the risks that are operative in any such intimate encounter, regardless of the safeguards and boundaries we install.

The levels of intimacy in a therapist's personal and professional lives may not coincide. Whereas most of us may be quite willing to let ourselves be close to our clients, we may not be so successful at committing ourselves to the intimacy of social and family relationships. Still, if we stay in the field long enough, we must eventually confront our reluctance and our defenses. One therapist admits with candor: "Being a therapist saved my life. I was about to go into the theater, which is most unhealthy and rewarded all the phony, manipulative, narcissistic parts of me. When I chose therapy it demanded that I deal with issues that I never would have changed in another environment. I made a choice for health."

The decision to work to improve the mental health of others is a choice to improve ourselves in the process. We must confront our own fears of intimacy and risk annihilation of our identity in every session with a client. We risk not only the submergence of our self in another but also continual confrontation with our own vulnerabilities.

Doing Good

The risks that come with the territory of being a therapist emanate primarily from getting so close to the flame that burns deep within the sorrow of each client we see. Yet in spite of the many hardships and occupational hazards of this work, we also experience tremendous satisfaction.

Altruism is certainly a driving force behind our motives and actions as helpers. There is nothing like that feeling of elation we sometimes experience when we know beyond a shadow of a doubt that our efforts have helped redeem a human life. Whether the result of a prolonged commitment to a relationship that spans years or a single gesture that yields immediate results, the joy we feel knowing that we have made a difference goes far beyond mere professional pride; sometimes this "helper's high" creates an incredible surge of tranquility, inner peace, and well-being (Luks, 1988).

I was walking down the street one day, lost in fantasies about what flavor of frozen yogurt I would have, when I saw a flash of color and movement ahead, accompanied by screams of indignation. I rushed to the scene and discovered two children, a girl of about seven and a boy of six, fighting on the sidewalk. The larger and stronger girl quickly dispatched her foe and then in triumph scattered the contents of his bookbag all over the street. Papers flew everywhere like mutant snowflakes, falling down and around this little boy, who was sobbing in frustrated helplessness.

I gathered up as many of his things as I could find, stooped down on my knees, and handed him his reloaded bag. He looked at me, startled at first by my intrusion into his misery. Then he broke out into the most glorious smile I had ever seen, and probably will ever see again. I felt his gratitude wash over me. As I continued on my journey, tears now ran down *my* face. I was just so thankful that I happened to be there at that moment so I could help him. I was able to do some good. In that simple interchange, lasting not more than two minutes, I had a relationship with another person that was helpful. In an infinitesimal way, that effort of "doing good" helped make the world a better place. During subsequent periods of frustration, I have thought about that little boy's smile, and somehow the risks and aggravation I must put up with have seemed worthwhile.

This is my most enduring image of what it means to be a therapist. Amidst the bureaucracy, paperwork, politics, finances, client resistance, and any personal side effects I feel from doing this kind of work, the greatest kick I get is from the realization that I said or did something, in isolation or as an accumulative effect, that made a difference to someone else. This desire to be useful is, in fact, the primary reason that most of us entered this profession in the first place (Guy, Stark, & Poelstra, 1987).

Therapist Self-Healing

For the most part, therapists live relatively flexible lives. Except for those therapists who work in corporate, government, or other large organizational settings, most therapists in universities, schools, community agencies, and especially private practice can exercise considerable control over their schedules and work priorities. Supervision and structure are usually minimal. Like the artist and musician, the therapist needs freedom to flourish and create.

The marriage between the personal and the professional in the life of a therapist is never clearer than in the benefits the career provides for its practitioners. Far beyond any monetary, prestige, or freedom needs that are satisfied are the opportunities for growth. "I practice psychotherapy not to rescue others from their craziness, but to preserve what is left of my own sanity: not to cure others, but to heal myself" (Kopp, 1985, p. 12). Just how does this self-healing take place?

We return to the mundane details of what a therapist actually does during the day, not only the dramatic moments of truth when a client finally understands and feels grateful but also the frustrations, repetitions, and stalemates. First of all, therapists have to sit still for long periods of time, and from this we learn physical self-discipline. Rivaling the most accomplished monk, a therapist develops phenomenal powers of focused concentration. We resist the intrusion of external distractions—cars honking, doors slamming, clocks ticking, uncrossed bare legs sitting across from us, phones ringing, unanswered messages winking—and, as though in a meditative trance, gently nudge our minds back into the present. With stoic self-control we ignore internal distractions—grumbling stomachs, unfinished conversations, undone errands, the past, the future—and return once again to the task at hand. From such deliberate and studied engrossment we develop a razor-sharp intellect that is only improved by the things we must learn to remain effective.

Therapists field questions like line drives during batting practice. We leap and duck, catch some and sidestep others. "When will I get better?" "Why do I hurt?" "How do you feel about me?" "What am I here for?" "How do I grow old?" "What should I do?" "What would you do?" Whether we respond to these questions aloud or not, we must nevertheless answer them—either then or later. We can flee, but there is nowhere to hide. Every working day holds for us a confrontation with the issues we fear most.

Every time we speak to our clients we heal ourselves, for there is an audience of two. We talk about what we know or what we think we know, but we teach only what we understand. We feel a tremendous incentive to answer life's most difficult questions and understand things and people. If we analyze the content of our sessions, regardless of clients' presenting symptoms, we will find our most disturbing themes and the things we best understand.

I take inventory of my case load. Tina is learning to stop thinking obsessively, or at least to stop obsessing about her obsessions. She has made progress in that now she only talks about her obsessions during therapy sessions. Whenever I try to get her to talk about something else, her symptoms spill over into her work and marriage. We have learned not to tamper with what is already working, even if it is sometimes boring to listen to. Tina has learned to accept and live with her irritating symptoms. From her I have learned to live with my irritating symptoms, too.

Michelle has taught me a lot about patience. After eighteen months together I finally gave up trying to control or structure our talks. Each week she tells me that something is bothering her, but she will not say what it is because she does not trust me. I complain that I cannot help her if she will not trust me. She says: "Fine. I'll go find someone else who won't require me to trust him." She keeps feeling better, but I cannot figure out why.

Feeling trapped in her marriage, Rachel used to cry the entire session. But now we play a wonderful game together. Each week she comes in having already decided to take on one of two parts. If she decides to be the dutiful but misunderstood wife, then I attempt to help her feel satisfied with the status quo. She then leaves the office resolved to initiate more open communication with her husband. But the harder she tries, the more frustrated she becomes. (The husband is only interested in his work, his model-T Ford, and thrice weekly in the missionary position.) Inevitably, she returns the following week prepared for divorce. We then discuss why she should follow that course of action, but we both know she will change her mind before the week has ended. Twice I attempted to confront her about this circular pattern, but she punished me for my impatience by canceling the next appointment.

These few cases are a profile in diversity familiar to most therapists. Yet there is also similarity in the issues clients confront—and repetition in the things we hear ourselves say again and again.

Taking Our Own Advice

Even the most creative, inventive, and impulsive clinician will teach similar lessons to all her clients. Our moral imperatives, favorite platitudes, and well-worn words of wisdom find their way into almost every session. Regardless of the client or presenting complaint, there is repetition in the themes we present.

- If you do not take care of yourself, nobody else will.
- We will be dead for a very long time.
- Symptoms are useful in getting your attention.
- Symptoms will not go away until they are no longer needed.
- We are all afraid to be alone.
- If you do not expect anything, you will never be disappointed.
- One hundred years from now nobody will care what you did with your life.

- The material world *is* seductive.
- Feeling powerless is a state of mind.
- We spend our lives trying to control our hormones.
- No matter what you do or say, half the world will like it and half the world will not.
- You will never have your parents' approval.
- You have less to lose than you think.
- We will never ever be content for very long.
- It is hard to love without vulnerability.
- Change does not occur without risks.
- We are all afraid of being wrong.
- We do not like the responsibility of being right.
- Everything worth doing is difficult.

If we only took our own advice more seriously! As Penzer (1984) notes: "I have often wondered as I sit in my office at 9:00 P.M. encouraging a father to spend more time with his son why he doesn't ask me what I am doing talking to him at this hour of the night. Nor do I enjoy the dissonance of spending several hours a day playing Uno, Checkers, and War in the name of play therapy and coming home in the evening and casting my children's requests aside in the name of fatigue" (p. 54).

We disregard our own advice not only by ignoring the messages we repeat but by failing to implement them in our lives. It hurts to be a hypocrite. Day after day we admonish clients for doing less than they are capable of, while an echoing voice nags at our conscience: "What have *you* done lately?" We critically help clients define those behaviors they would most like to change and end up doing likewise for ourselves. How can we expect clients to understand ideas we have not fully mastered?

It is the ultimate hypocrisy of our profession that we do not or cannot do the same things we ask of our students and clients. How many professors, therapist educators, and supervisors do you know who teach the importance of warmth, caring, respect, and authenticity in therapeutic relationships but are aloof, mistrustful, controlling, and manipulative in their own relationships? How many practitioners and educators do you know who "preach" the importance of compassion and reciprocal giving yet are themselves narcissistic and self-indulgent?

We were critical of some of our mentors, supervisors, and teachers who abused us, who were hypocritical in not being able to do the things they asked us to do. "As much as we promised ourselves that *we* would never become what we most despised—pompous, arrogant, monotonous, or self-obsessed—it is frightening to consider just how much we may be perceived in exactly those ways by the current generation of neophytes (who are now telling themselves that *they* will never become like us)" (Kottler, 1992b, p. 476).

Therapists naturally do many other things that lead to self-healing. Out of necessity we are good at valuing and organizing our time. Because of our training and exposure to the consequences of self-neglect we have an elevated capacity to perceive our own stress. We thus remain sensitized to certain warning signs, such as sleep disruption or excuse making or agitation or something in the body and mind feeling out of balance. Once these potential problems are identified we can immediately take steps to correct them. Therapists work with colleagues who happen to be experts at giving support and nurturance. From the perspective of human contact, we work in an enriched environment. In theory, anyway, our professional relationships should offer the potential for personal fulfillment. There should be opportunities for constructive feedback, for benevolent guidance, and for lots of hugs.

Unfortunately, there is often a discrepancy between what should be and what actually is. Therapists can be as cruel, manipulative, insensitive, self-involved, and political as the rest of the human race. Fortunately, we are trained to deal with deception, game playing, and politics with minimal threat to the self.

Things We Learn

Perhaps the greatest benefit of practicing therapy is what we learn on a daily basis. Each client brings with him the sum total of his accumulated knowledge, and his primary job is to share the context of his life, complete with all relevant background information. We are thus offered a glimpse into the most intimate world of humanity. We learn about the customs, language, and culture of diverse ethnic groups. We are exposed to differences in Italian, Chaldean, Indian, Jewish, African-American, or American Indian family structures. We learn about religions, unique foods, and even the most intimate details of sexual and social behavior.

In the story of his journey as a therapist with five clients who attended his group and individual sessions Bugental (1990) operates from the assumption that he learns as much from his clients as they learn from him. While reflecting on the lessons that clients teach their therapists, Bugental realized that what he considers most important to know and understand he learned doing therapy: that choice is power, that perfectionism is a disease, that relationships are terrifying, that loss is a part of life, that just as clients imprison themselves and their worlds so are we guilty of limiting our own choices and possibilities.

As we immerse ourselves in our clients' lives, we also spend much time learning what people do for work. We learn not only about conventional careers but also about those on the fringe of society. In any given week we may learn about life as a professional athlete, politician, engineer, prostitute, or factory worker. As a by-product of our therapeutic digging, we find out the most interesting details of how corporate decisions are made, how drug deals are consummated, how a poem is created, how clothing is most easily stolen, what waiters secretly do to customers they do not like, how the stock market works, how a tennis player trains, how someone is really elected to office, how an assembly worker copes with boredom on the line, how a seventh grader tries to win friends and influence people, how an advertising writer thinks up ideas, how a policeman controls his aggressive urges, and how another therapist deals with burnout.

One particularly fascinating area of human activity that

is accessible to us is what people do when they are alone. I do not mean the usual nose picking or masturbating, but the diverse range of behaviors and activities that occupy people's time when nobody else is around. We learn about people who lack self-esteem and solid defenses, who are so afraid of being alone that they will do almost anything for distraction. We meet the exercise fanatics, the ultramarathoners who run for two to three hours a day. Some people use books as an escape; for others, drugs work even better.

I systematically investigated and categorized the diversity of activities that people engage in when they are alone, a subject that is accessible only to therapists (Kottler, 1990). We hear about the wonderfully strange fantasies that people act out, their solitary rituals, the things they say and do when nobody is watching. We have not only permission to pry into clients' private moments but a mandate to do so. We learn about human beings at their most playful, spontaneous, creative, uninhibited, and self-destructive.

We have the privilege of knowing what people really think, feel, and do when their guard is down. And we get paid for it. Not only does the information we gain from clients help us better understand them; such knowledge also helps us better understand ourselves. Steinzor (1972, p. 183) comments: "Such vicarious pleasures do much to help me accommodate to lives I can never live. Yet these unsolicited, unintended gifts also provide the context for the continuous rearousal and reinterpretation of my own anguish."

The work of the therapist can be so interesting and so

personally relevant as well as professionally satisfying that I sometimes (but not for very long) feel the urge to pay my clients for what they teach me. Yet it takes incredible energy to do good therapy. Thus I both resent and feel grateful for the incentive to constantly challenge myself.

Not only do therapists learn from their clients, but therapists' personal curiosity often complements their professional inquiry. The training programs of therapists, whether in medicine, education, psychology, or social work, emphasize an interdisciplinary perspective to integrate the study of mind and body. Biochemistry is a prerequisite for understanding the organic basis of many emotional disorders as well as the actions of psychopharmacological medication. Neurophysiology is necessary for the differential diagnosis of psychosomatic illnesses. Sociology, social psychology, sociobiology, and social anthropology help explain the social context of symptoms. Educational psychology provides theories of learning and development that we use for facilitating healthy growth. Philosophy and general systems theory help the therapist reason logically, organize knowledge, and formulate coherent explanations for physical and spiritual phenomena.

Freud found the fiction of Dostoyevsky, Sophocles, and Shakespeare; the sculpture of Michelangelo and Leonardo; the philosophy of Mill and Nietzsche to be the inspiration for his theories. It was not his formal medical training as much as his readings of *King Lear, Hamlet, Oedipus Rex*, and *The Brothers Karamazov* that formed the cornerstone of his theories. Freud was first and foremost an integrationist who was able to draw on the wisdom of poets, sculptors, neurologists, philosophers, playwrights, and his patients to create a unified vision of the human world.

In the tradition of Freud, many of his disciples educated themselves as generalists with influences from diverse academic disciplines. Jung, for example, was heavily influenced by his Latin and theological studies, as well as by the philosophy of Goethe, Schopenhauer, and Kant and by the practitioners of the new science of psychiatry. Rollo May, the North American champion of existentialism, described perhaps the most pragmatic recipe for a style of therapy that used ingredients from philosophy (Kierkegaard, Nietzsche, Heidegger), psychoanalysis (Freud), phenomenology (Merleau-Ponty, Husserl), art (Cézanne, van Gogh), theology (Marcel, Jaspers), literature (Sartre, Camus, Kafka), and the concentration camps (Frankl). There is, therefore, great historical precedent in our field for learning as much as we can about everything. Ours is a science of experience, not only from formal research and case conferences but from literature, that aids our understanding of the complexities of emotion and behavior. Without Shakespeare's plays, Dostoyevsky's novels, or James's short stories, our knowledge of anguish and conflict would be hollow, our self-revelations one-dimensional.

Uses and Abuses of Self-Disclosure

Personal and professional issues most clearly intersect in the decision concerning how much to disclose during sessions. If the therapist is reserved and aloof, she risks alienating the client and creating interactions that could become wooden and stale. If she is too open and self-revealing, she risks diminishing the client's importance.

The problem is not so much whether to reveal oneself, since a therapist's unique personality will permeate sessions anyway, but whether to capitalize on the effects systematically. Basescu (1990) reports, for example, on several specific instances when he may use self-disclosure: to create a more co-equal relationship, to communicate caring, to encourage more open disclosures on the part of the client, to acknowledge the therapeutic relationship as a fully human encounter, to validate client experiences, and to illustrate key points through personal examples. But it is never, *never* to be used to meet one's personal needs.

The value of self-disclosure is reported by Polster (1972) in his experiences as a client with Fritz Perls. At first, like most people, he was enamored of Perls's flamboyance but noticed that Perls could be very tough and cutting. He found Perls intimidating and unapproachable, and so he remained passive, withdrawn, and silent during group sessions. During a break, Perls took him aside and related the story of his own fear of speaking in public, which had plagued him until a few years earlier. For Polster, this was a breakthrough: "I was amazed and felt the gift he was giving me" (p. 154). In later sessions he was able to share knowing that even (and especially) the leader could empathize.

By revealing part of herself, the therapist indicates her emotional involvement in the sessions. The decision to reveal oneself to clients is not made solely on the basis of their need to know us as a real person. "It also results from the therapist's need to be a real person and to interact with another person in a reciprocating manner" (Guy, 1987, p. 141). With respect to several significant events in a therapist's life — marriage, divorce, pregnancy, parenthood, relocation, illness, death of a loved one, aging — Guy describes the dilemma we face: to withhold such major life transitions from the client is to deny that we are anything other than objects; yet in disclosing them we risk becoming self-indulgent, sidetracking the focus of sessions. It is his conclusion that a forthright discussion of obvious changes in our lives is not only helpful but crucial to maintaining the integrity of the therapeutic relationship.

This sharing can be among the most powerful tools to encourage further sharing by the client (Jourard, 1971). When used in a timely and restrained manner, such self-disclosure can build a more authentic (Bugental), congruent (Rogers), transparent (Jourard), genuine (Carkhuff), and open (Kaiser) relationship (Curtis, 1982). Of course, certain kinds of self-disclosure work better than others, depending on their timing and function and the degree to which they provide valuable feedback to the client as well as contribute to *constructive* intimacy in the relationship (Derlega, Hendrick, Winstead, & Berg, 1991).

Kopp (1972) describes the illustrious history of masters instructing their pilgrims primarily by disclosing themselves. The mystics, monks, masters, ancient philosophers, healers, and teachers all promoted growth through their personal parables. "When I work with a patient, not only will I be hearing his tale, but I shall be telling him mine as well. If we are to get anywhere, we must come to know one another. One of the luxuries of being a psychotherapist is that it helps to keep you honest. It's a bit like remaining in treatment all of your life. It helps me to remain committed to telling and retelling my tale for the remainder of that pilgrimage that is my life" (p. 17).

Yet there are few therapeutic activities that are so abused under the guise of being helpful. Excessive self-disclosure may be done to relieve the therapist's own discomfort with the inherent inequality of the relationship (Herron & Rouslin, 1984). Afterwards, it is easy to find some clinical justification: "I'm only trying to make the client feel comfortable" or "I thought he might feel less alone in his pain" or "I am only being real." If self-disclosure is not moderated, all the barriers between the personal and the professional become muddled, and the client's fundamental perceptions of therapist competence and empathy may be irrevocably altered (Curtis, 1982). Transference is also sacrificed when the therapist relinquishes his nonpersonhood in favor of an authentic relationship.

Yalom (1980) believes that personal concealment for the sake of transference only denies the client the opportunity to experience a more genuine, loving encounter. These sentiments are also echoed by Anna Freud (1954) who felt that room should be made for the realization that the analyst and the patient are two real people of equal adult status and are in a real relationship to each other.

Whether at the lecture podium, in the media, or when writing, teaching, or counseling, self-disclosure is most effective when the therapist adheres to a personally developed set of standards that best bring out her personality with professional restraint. We wish to communicate our warmth, authenticity, and distinct humanness without diminishing our authority, expertise, and power. Such a balance can be reached if the practitioner asks herself a few questions.

- What do I hope this will accomplish?
- Is there another way of making the same point?
- What do I risk by not sharing myself?
- To what extent am I attempting to meet my own needs?
- Is this the right time?
- How can I say this most concisely?
- How will the client personalize what I share about myself?
- How can I put the focus back on the client?

Certainly there is little time to consider these self-queries in the instant before we speak. Nevertheless, such a vigilant attitude should be developed in order to avoid the narcissistic lapses possible for those crossing the professional-personal barrier. Whenever we give away any part of ourselves, clients feel grateful, although they may sometimes stop to consider why. We can be most helpful by presenting to them only those parts of ourselves that help them see themselves more clearly.

Personal Fallout

In addition to the usual countertransference reactions a therapist experiences in response to client behavior and issues, when we work with families or groups of clients we also must contend with an enmeshed, multiperson system that is potentially unpredictable and explosive. The group/family therapist must deal with more acting out in response to his being in an authority role and must simultaneously deal with myriad feelings and reactions to each person in the group as well as to the group members' interactive patterns.

Tina catches my eye and smiles in a flirtatious way. I feel flattered, then uncomfortable and guarded. I notice that Fred sees the little interchange and smirks. Tina smiles at him, too. I feel a little jealous about that, then chagrined that I am irritated with Fred. At that moment Cassie pipes up with another distracting question. I am tired of her insensitivity and so confront her. Tina rushes in to defend her, so I turn to her. I realize, just before I am about to confront her as well, that I am still haunted by her earlier flirtatious gesture.

I have now lost the threads of where we were headed. I feel overwhelmed by how much there is to attend to and all the complex and varied reactions I have to each person in the group, how they relate to one another and to me. These effects do not end once the group ends but continue to plague me throughout the week.

We try to keep a vigilant eye on personal fallout to protect our family and friends from the intensity of our professional life. Yet with all the restraint we must exercise in order to follow the rules regulating our conduct during working hours, it is difficult to not be abusive, surly, or self-indulgent with our loved ones. All day long we have stifled ourselves, censored our thoughts and statements, and disciplined ourselves to be controlled and intelligent. And then we make an abrupt transition to go home. Much of the pressure that has been building all day long as clients have come in and dumped their troubles finally releases as we walk through the door. If we are not careful, our families will suffer the emotional fallout.

The final interchange between the personal and the professional in the life of a therapist has its impact in the amount of time we spend in self-reflection. After all the training we received in psychodiagnostics, recognizing defense mechanisms, perceiving things as they are, defusing game playing, we are creatures exquisitely designed to smell self-deception and set things right — not just when the meter is running during therapy, but instinctively when we are alone. Even if we do not deliberately keep track of how our work is currently affecting our emotional health, or how our personal life is affecting our therapy, such an evaluation will take place effortlessly. We find ourselves feeling self-conscious in a social situation, feel our hearts beating quickly, and immediately start talking to ourselves the way we would to a client. Or we make an interpretation during a session that is obviously off the mark and then begin to question what inside us led our clinical judgment astray.

The content of our therapeutic metaphors comes from

our personal experience. Much of what we say to clients is strongly influenced by what we have read and seen, who we have encountered, and what we have done that very week. I read a bedtime story to my son and the image of *The Giving Tree* (Silverstein, 1964) follows me into talks with a narcissistic client. Another person complains in anguish of feeling trapped, and I find myself describing a moving passage from *Ironweed* (Kennedy, 1983). I plant trees over the weekend and weave together for a disoriented young man an example of how each living thing requires nourishment, minimal shocks to the system during transplanting, and individual attention. The places I visit, the weather, dreams, memories — everything that filters through my senses affects what I do during sessions. My work in any given moment is the product of who I have become up to that very instant. As I change so does the style of my therapy.

We, like our clients, change only at a pace with which we are comfortable. If we move too quickly, with a client or with ourselves, the personal fallout reaches dangerous levels. Yet it takes such incredible energy and commitment not to lose ground, much less change one's position. We move just as fast as we can.

> *"Now! Now!" cried the Queen. "Faster! Faster!" And they went so fast that at last they seemed to skim through the air, hardly touching the ground with their feet, till suddenly, just as Alice was getting quite exhausted, they stopped, and she found herself sitting on the ground, breathless and giddy.*

> *The Queen propped her up against a tree, and said kindly, "You may rest a little now."*
>
> *Alice looked round her in great surprise. "Why, I do believe we've been under this tree the whole time! Everything's just as it was!"*
>
> *"Of course it is," said the Queen. "What would you have it?"*
>
> *"Well, in* our *country," said Alice, still panting a little, "you'd generally get to somewhere else — if you ran very fast for a long time as we've been doing."*
>
> *"A slow sort of country!" said the Queen. "Now HERE, you see, it takes all the running you can do, to keep in the same place. If you want to get somewhere else, you must run at least twice as fast as that!" [Carroll, (1871) 1981, p. 127].*

We all run just as fast as we can, although we sometimes seem to stay in the same place, reworking the same issues again and again. In a typical psychiatric clinic, a dozen colleagues were asked how their values, old baggage, and new dreams influence their style of helping. One psychologist lost her mother to cancer while still a child and somehow finds a way to diagnose all psychopathology as a form of mother-child deprivation. She views her primary role as providing the maternal nurturance that she herself so longs for. A social worker has had great difficulty dealing with authority and anger. Not coincidentally, he specializes in work with adolescents who inappropriately act out their hostility. Another psychologist has struggled since childhood with obsessive thinking and her fear of going crazy. In her practice she requests the most disturbed referrals and prefers working with psychotic disorders. A family counselor prizes humor and spontaneity above all other human experiences and so functions as a court jester to make people laugh. Such a correlation between the major themes of our personal lives and our professional style of practice is something most of us can identify with. Despite our best efforts to separate the two roles, the barrier remains permeable.

The Human Dimensions
of Being a Therapist

I recognize the compatibility between the personal and professional in my own life for a number of reasons. First and foremost, it makes my work more fun. I find greater meaning in everything I do when I can relate it to the rest of my life. I like the feeling that I am always working, always thinking, and always trying to make sense of what is happening, and yet I am never working since even time spent with clients helps me to learn more about the world and myself. Second, I monitor the interaction between my personal and professional lives to protect both my clients and my family. I know I have unresolved personal issues that get in the way of my being more effective with my clients. I must constantly guard against my self-indulgences, egocentricity, and narcissism. I frequently catch myself saying and doing things in sessions for my own entertainment. I ask questions only to satisfy my curiosity. I let clients dig themselves into holes just to see how they will get out. I inflate my sense of importance so clients will admire me more. I probably see clients longer than is absolutely necessary because I need the money. Oh, I justify all of these actions, convincing myself they are all for the client's good. I do not worry as much about this personal fallout because I am aware of it. I do genuinely worry about those instances when I do not catch myself meeting my own needs.

In all of these factors that connect the personal with the professional, the therapist is seen as a complex being with conflicting desires and multiple urges motivated by altruism, egocentricity, and self-interest. It is difficult, if not impossible, to filter personal elements out of a therapist's professional work, or to restrict clinical perceptions and skills to the office. "I believe the notion of 'therapeutic detachment' is an oxymoron, a self-deception, and a seduction for the faint-hearted" (Bugental, 1990, p. xvii). Henry, Sims, and Spray (1973) and other researchers only confirm what most practitioners know intuitively: that our therapeutic perspective on life is our greatest asset and greatest liability. Being a therapist affords us the opportunity for continual spiritual, intellectual, and emotional growth. We become more intuitive, better risk takers and communicators. We experience excitement, human intensity, confidence, and self-fulfillment, all at great expense. The consuming nature of therapeutic work reminds us of a universal truth we so often repeat to clients: every joy has its price, whether we pay now or on the installment plan.

chapter 4

HARDSHIPS OF
THERAPEUTIC PRACTICE

*t*he marriage between the personal and the professional in the life of a therapist provides not only an enriched form of work but also some special hardships. The clinician's life is fraught with draining days, intense pressures, and personal risks. Those who become too involved in their work pay a dear price in giving up leisure time and a private life; those who too assertively distance themselves from therapeutic sessions risk emotional sterility in other relationships.

Ours is a life of mobility. The turnover and burnout rates of therapists functioning in organized mental health settings are frightening. Those in private practice switch clinic affiliations as they would cars. Temptations of more money or power, a roomier office, or more freedom lure practitioners in a game of musical chairs. If you stay too long in one place, colleagues begin to wonder why you do not leave.

The various specialties within therapy present their special stresses and problems. In addition to the hazards associated with seeing clients and functioning within an organization, each practitioner must confront identity problems he inherited with his training. As we all know, status, power, competence, and expertise are not divided equally among the specialties practicing therapy. Psychiatrists, for example, must contend with their lack of early training in therapy and an orientation toward the medical model that brands them among fellow physicians as quacks who do not do anything and among their nonmedical colleagues as pill-doctors who try to do too much.

Many social workers struggle with the obsolete public image of those in their profession as do-gooders who chat with people in their homes. Within the mental health network they fight for parity with psychologists, who have their own problems trying to prove what they can do best. Psychiatric nurses and mental health counselors quietly go about their therapeutic work, but they are often frustrated by their lack of recognition. Each clinician, regardless of her chosen specialty and work setting, carries a tremendous burden into a therapy session before the client even opens his mouth.

Special Problems of Beginners

Therapists-in-training shoulder additional burdens related to their fears of inadequacy and avoidance of failure. They are under competitive academic pressure at the same time they are struggling to develop a professional identity and to reconcile some of the paradoxes of their profession — to get close but not *too* close to clients, to be caring yet detached, to provide support without fostering dependency, and the ultimate mystery: how it is possible for so many of their professors and supervisors to be equally effective in their work even though they appear to be doing such different things.

Perhaps most stressful of all for neophytes is reconciling the discrepant feedback they receive. Present a case — *any* case — to a collection of peers, and watch the show that ensues. I was completely stuck with a young woman who had been deteriorating after showing an initial surge of progress. A crucial point in our work together centered on the ambivalence she felt toward men. She had as yet been unable to consummate sexual intercourse because of an inability to lubricate sufficiently, perhaps even because of vaginismus, or tightening of the vaginal muscles. Why, she asked me at a critical juncture, if I am so afraid of penetration, is my most frequent fantasy of being raped?

A good question. An *excellent* question. Unfortunately, I had no earthly idea. Because I could not think of what else to do, I did what any self-respecting therapist in my position would do — I stalled and put the focus on her until I could get some help: "That is a good question. What do *you* think it means?"

We hemmed and hawed for a while. The session ended with the resolve that we would explore the issue in greater depth next time. The moment she walked out the door, I cornered a tribunal of my peers. "Okay, guys, here is the situation. What the heck does this mean?"

Another issue involved here was my feeling of inadequacy: if I were really a good therapist, I would know what this means. This uneasiness was only reinforced by my colleagues' easy assurance that they understood this phenomenon. What confounds me to this day is that each of their interpretations was different!

"She was obviously sexually abused. You checked this out, didn't you?"

Before I could reply, another chimed in: "I would think she has fears of intimacy. I would reframe this as a relationship problem rather than a sexual issue."

I took notes furiously. That last one sounded good, until the next suggestion, and the next one, and the one after that. I heard five different suggestions for the same case. I wondered how a doctor would proceed if he or she asked five colleagues to examine a patient and they came up with five different diagnoses and treatments.

This discrepant feedback we get from superiors, colleagues, and books we read only adds to the confusion, uncertainty, and stress we live with. We face people every day who want answers, and we do our best to appease their needs for certainty. But all the while we have our own doubts — feelings of uneasiness that are often made worse by the sheer diversity of ideas that flourish in our field — all with a devoted following.

Take, for example, the predicament that many therapists find themselves in whereby they must satisfy not only their clients as consumers of their services but also the expectations of their supervisors. Even more potentially stressful is the fact that most practitioners answer to more than one supervisor; rarely are they in complete agreement as to what to do in a given situation.

Being concerned with the effects of discrepant feedback on beginners in the field, I conducted a little study on how different supervisors would react to the same situation. I took a typescript of a session conducted by an intern and distributed it to members of a counselor education faculty. It is not unusual as a training device to require beginners to do a complete typescript of a session so that written feedback can be provided on each intervention. What happens, however, when a therapist receives discrepant, even contradictory feedback on the same behavior? One supervisor tells you to confront, another to reflect feelings. Certainly that creates a stressful predicament. One especially promising therapist found herself at an internship site where her supervisors were rotated every two weeks. She eventually was hospitalized for "nervous exhaustion."

After distributing the typescript to the faculty, I asked them to write down any feedback they had for the student. Here is one excerpt from the session, a client statement, the counselor's subsequent response, and then seven different supervisor comments that were written in the margin.

>   *Client: "Nobody can believe that the state de-*
>   *partment requires seventy-one credits beyond a*
>   *bachelor's degree to get a license to teach elemen-*
>   *tary school."*
>   *Counselor: "Now, you weren't sure you even*

wanted to teach because you want to teach students that were willing and interested in learning."

Supervisor 1: Good direction but awkwardly worded.

Supervisor 2: Why did you say that?

Supervisor 3: This confrontation seems premature.

Supervisor 4: I am unsure of what you are trying to do here.

Supervisor 5: Good restatement.

Supervisor 6: This statement appears unwarranted.

Supervisor 7: Excellent response! You are moving the client closer to the real issue.

This diversity of feedback highlights the pressures we are under in trying to make sense of what clients are presenting to us at the same time we are sorting out a dozen different suggestions from our colleagues.

Occupational Hazards

It was Freud ([1937] 1950) who first suggested that therapists submit themselves for further treatment every five years because of the regressive effects caused by constant contact with clients' emotionally charged issues. Freud moved his clients to the couch primarily because he could not stand looking at them all the time. That such a reclining position facilitated free association was incidental.

In the face of incredible emotional arousal — anger, sadness, panic, despondency, conflict — the therapist is expected to maintain neutrality, detachment, frustration tolerance, empathy, alertness, interest, and impulse control without feeling depleted, deprived, and isolated (Bellack & Faithorn, 1981). As if such demands are not enough, we are also supposed to be charming and invigorated by the time we get home. Since our friends and family know what we do for a living, they have greater expectations that we will be inhumanly patient, forgiving, and compromising during those instances when they have us locked in battle.

One social worker has worked for the state department of social services for twelve years. She is completely entrenched in the system — politically, emotionally, and financially. She is also cynical, aloof, and sarcastic. Her job description as senior clinician sounds as though it were written by a naive, altruistic academic. There is little time to spend with her clients since most of her energy is devoted to keeping her position in the ever-changing power hierarchy. She is afraid of the abused women she must treat — they seem so pathetic and remind her too much of the way she feels. She commutes forty-five minutes into the city each day, replaces the hubcaps on her car as they vanish into that place where hubcaps go, and is patiently waiting for eighteen more years to pass so she can retire. She feels old at thirty-four. She has seen too much of man's inhumanity to man. She has nightmares about broken people without hope; she sees the faces of children dotted with cigarette burns. She cannot leave the system since she has a vested interest in the retirement plan. Besides, where would she go?

A psychologist teaches at the university and consults with local mental health agencies. His professional life is varied as he routinely switches roles from researcher to teacher to clinician to administrator. He did not perish in the struggle to publish. He is well-respected by his colleagues, feared by his students, and admired by his clients, who understand little of what he says. He has carefully nurtured his reputation in the community. As time goes on, his lecture notes become frayed, their folders yellow. Each year he gets older, but he continues to meet the stony faces of students who are always nineteen. If they have talked to friends who had him last semester, they have already heard his best jokes and learned the answers to the final exam. He has taught the educational psychology class thirty-seven times. Thirty-seven times he has heard himself say, "Welcome to Ed Psych. There will be two examinations..." wondering what this has to do with learning about helping people. Students rarely come to visit, so he spends much of his time in the university senate or on departmental, curriculum excellence, and promotional review committees. For fun he waits for his sabbatical once every seven years so he can catch up on all the computer data that have been piling up on his bookshelves.

A psychiatrist in private practice appears to have the best of all worlds—a lucrative and successful case load, freedom, self-employment, self-direction, status, and power. Yet he is trapped by his own ambition and greed. He conducts fifty-five sessions per week, neglecting his health, family, and leisure pursuits in order to gross $250,000 per year. What is there to envy? His accountant puts him in limited partnership real estate ventures to shelter his income. As long as he maintains his productivity he will make out like a bandit on his tax returns. But if his income falls, he will have wasted all his energy. His capital is tied up in investments. His cash flow is dependent on his earnings. The tax shelters are useless unless he can sustain or increase his income. He cannot take a vacation without feeling guilty. He grudgingly decides to spend a week in Bermuda but occupies himself figuring out that the hours he is spending lying on the beach are costing him $500 in lost income — plus his expenses. He cannot wait to get back to his office.

A marriage and family therapist, who splits her time between contract work for a community agency and a part-time private practice, feels like she is always looking for more work. A single parent with complete financial responsibility for her children, she can never quite get on a solid footing. Most of the families and couples she works with cannot afford her full fees, so her sliding scale has slid below what she can afford to live on. There was a time when she loved doing family therapy, but now it feels to her as if she is underpaid, unappreciated, and overstressed. She feels torn when a couple cancels — finally an hour to recover from her previous sessions of the day, yet when she does not work, she is not paid for her time. She thinks seriously about taking on a third part-time job, just for a little while to make ends meet.

The preceding examples of how a few professionals experience the hardships of therapy portray only a minority of therapists, and certainly very few of those readers who would ever purchase and read a book on the personal consequences of practicing therapy. Nevertheless, we all know practitioners who have let the side effects of therapeutic work really get to them. We shudder at the thought that it could be happening to us at this very moment. And what is the "it" that infects the nervous systems of people who try to help others for a living? How do our clients get to us, unravel our precious control, haunt us with their fears?

Sleepless Nights

Clients bring us their nightmares, drop them in our laps, and then leave us to sort them out for ourselves. They have been enduring sleepless nights for years. Now the challenge for us is to keep away their demons. Especially at night, when we are relaxed and our defenses are down, images creep into our dreams, or if we are lying awake, they invade our peace. We toss and turn, probably in synchrony with the very client who infected us.

Novelist Jim Harrison (1984, p. 17) describes a night I remember poignantly but prefer not to repeat.

Insomnia opens the door to previously untraced memories, makes a mockery of the good sense that possesses one at high noon, and any effort we make to channel our thoughts twists the energy, rebukes

*us with half-finished faces, sexless bodies; we learn
again that our minds are full of snares, knots,
goblins, the backward march of the dead, the
bridges that end halfway and still hang in the air,
those who failed to love us, those who irreparably
harmed us, intentionally or not, even those we hurt
badly and live on incapsulated in our regret. The
past thrives on a sleepless night, reduces it to the
awesome, distorted essence of all we have met.*

Any client's story could be the trigger, but there is usually one particularly sad or terrifying tale that returns to haunt us when we are alone in the dark. We tell ourselves it was someone else's misery, but by then it is too late: the chain reaction has started, and we are probing deeply into our own failures.

One image brought to me by a client will haunt me until I die. Even though I had read stories and seen movies about this sort of thing, I could never have been prepared for the intensity I would feel being so close to someone who had been really terrorized. One day, when the client was living in a faraway city, she ran into an old high school friend who was on vacation. Although he was more of an acquaintance than a good friend, she nevertheless knew him quite well since he had been her senior class president. They were delighted to run into each other after so much time and in such a large city. They stopped to have coffee, to chat, and to catch up on their lives. Then they parted ways. She went back to her apartment and, as was her habit, read stories to her little girl until she fell asleep and then began studying at her desk. Several hours later there was a knock at the door. She asked who it was and heard her high school friend's voice say that he had brought something she had forgotten. As her hand hovered over the handle she saw her daughter standing in her bedroom doorway. She was momentarily distracted as she swung open the door and turned to see her friend with a disfigured, hideous grin on his face and a butcher knife raised in each hand. Although she eventually recovered from her wounds, she would never again open a door without taking some evasive action. And she has never since had a peaceful night.

It has been a while since I heard this story. I still hesitate before I open doors to strangers. And late at night I see the hideous faces from my past coming at me with big knives.

Sources of Stress

Many therapists are heard to say that if only they could be left alone to do their real work—the business of seeing clients—and insulated from the politics of their organizations, their lives would be greatly enriched. The sad fact is, however, that many of our staff support groups are like extremely dysfunctional families. Power struggles go on behind the scenes. We are constantly triangulated into conflicts with peers and supervisors that drain our energy and demoralize us. All too often what is best for clients takes a backseat to the posturing of our most insecure colleagues. The demands of insurance companies pressure us to compromise treatment planning for the sake of economic realities.

Whereas our working environments ought to be a source of support, nurturance, and growth, too often we attempt to function effectively in spite of daily frustrations. In one private practice setting the therapists spend more time discussing how to beat the system and keep up their billings than they do planning ways to help their clients. In a community mental health center staff members spend their free time griping about budget cuts, supervisors' ineptitude, and nonsensical rules. A group of school counselors and social workers lament to one another that they never help kids anymore because they are so locked into their scheduling and administrative duties. Staff members at a university counseling center complain that they cannot do their jobs properly because of a lack of support among administrators who view their services as "nonessential."

In each of these cases the professionals spend almost as much time dealing with bureaucratic obstacles placed in their way as they do getting on with their clinical responsibilities. The usual pressures they experience as a result of their clinical work are exacerbated by additional obstacles. The result is an alarming burnout rate and distress level within our profession.

Three-quarters of practicing therapists have experienced significant distress during the past three years (Guy, Poelstra, & Stark, 1988). In their study of a small sample of prominent practitioners, Norcross and Guy (1989) found a similar incidence of personal stress. Time pressures were cited as the most frequently occurring precipitant of strain, although organizational politics, excessive workload, and conflicts with colleagues were also mentioned frequently.

From these studies as well as others (Deutsch, 1985; Elkind, 1992; Norcross & Prochaska, 1986) and from my own interviews with practitioners in the field, I have compiled the following list of sources of stress for therapists.

Client-Induced Stress	*Work Environment Stress*
angry outbursts	time pressures
accusations of	organizational politics
incompetence	rules and restrictions on
intense depression	freedom
suicidal threats or attempts	nonsupportive peers
triangulation into family	supervisory incompetence
premature termination	excessive paperwork
major deterioration	torn allegiances

Self-Induced Stress	*Event-Related Stress*
feelings of perfectionism	legal actions
ruminating about cases	money pressures
need for approval	major life transition
self-doubt	(divorce, relocation,
physical exhaustion	and so on)
unhealthy life-style	change in job
emotional depletion	responsibilities
excessive responsibility	economic cutbacks
for clients' welfare	

A pattern of distress is emerging from each of these sources of stress, one that includes psychological symptoms (boredom, isolation, frustration, irritability, depression), behavioral symptoms (procrastination, substance abuse, lowered productivity, recklessness), and physical symptoms (sleep disruption, appetite gain or loss, headaches, respiratory problems, muscular tension) (Rice, 1992). It appears as if the restraint and concentration we continually must exercise take their toll on our mental and physical health. We develop so many of the same symptoms that plague our clients, only we are better than they are at denial. Not only do our bodies and minds suffer, but so do our relationships.

One-Way Intimacy

Kovacs (1976) considered the tragic flaw of most therapists to be not the need for intimacy but its avoidance. Only within the sterile, ritualized context of a therapeutic session, where the clinician is both boss and observer, can he feel safe. There the therapist can experience loving relationships but can avoid the risks associated with real family conflict. Rollo May (Cunningham, 1985) speculates that one reason why people become therapists is because they are used to assuming that role in their families. Henry, Sims, and Spray (1973) discovered in their study of therapists that the great majority of their families were conflict ridden, and Burton (1972) found in his sample of famous clinicians that most had experienced great pain or illness in childhood. Whether we actually got started in the helping profession to save the world, to save our families, or to save ourselves, we enjoy getting close to others and helping to solve their problems. Yet the intimacy a therapist experiences with clients is strange. There are rules and structures, even payment for attention.

The major source of complaints to professional ethics committees and state licensing boards involves alleged sexual intimacies between clients and therapists. Researching the patterns of these incidents, Pope and Bouhoutsos (1986) identified a number of common types, including the "Svengali" scenario, in which the therapist creates and exploits client dependencies. Others include (1) "as if," wherein the therapist confuses transference with infatuation, (2) "it just got out of hand," in which emotional closeness grew beyond manageable limits, (3) "true love," or its rationalization as a justification for abandoning professional boundaries, (4) "time out," in which the therapist makes an arbitrary distinction that what occurs outside the office does not count, and (5) "hold me," in which erotic contact escalates from comfort gestures. In all of these cases, sexual involvement results from the high level of intimacy that makes *both* participants more vulnerable to counterproductive entanglements.

Malpractice suits against therapists for sexual misconduct are skyrocketing. Despite the indignation of a number of professionals who justifiably condemn such client abuse, it is easy to see how it could happen, especially since 87 percent of practicing therapists admit to feeling sexually attracted to their clients (Pope, Keith-Spiegel, & Tab-achnick, 1986). In Fitzgerald's *Tender Is the Night* (1933, p. 174), the patient confronts her therapist.

> *"You like me?"*
>
> *"Of course."*
>
> *"Would you —"* They were strolling along toward the dim end of the horseshoe, two hundred yards ahead. *"If I hadn't been sick would you — I mean, would I have been the sort of girl you might have — oh, slush, you know what I mean."*
>
> *He was in for it now, possessed by a vast irrationality. She was so near that he felt his breathing change but again his training came to his aid in a boy's laugh and a trite remark.*

Dr. Diver loses the struggle to keep his distance. The boundaries crumble in a searing kiss. They marry. Divorce. He vanishes into obscurity. Tender is the night, but, oh, so cruel is the blinding light of day. And we are reminded once again of the fragile front we try so hard to maintain. To love someone unconditionally, nonpossessively, nonsexually, with warmth, empathy, and genuineness, is exhausting.

We become for our clients not only objects of transference but live, breathing, loving, attractive people. Our clients' friends and spouses pale in comparison to our unconditional acceptance and professional relationship-building skills. We are rarely angry, irritable, short-tempered, or demanding. Instead we demonstrate only compassion, patience, wisdom, and control. Our clients feel attraction and gratitude. Some people, especially those who may find themselves in therapy, want to show their affection with their genitals.

And so we understand how a client might be motivated to conquer sexually a powerful, attractive model who also may be a reminder of prior unresolved relationships. What then of the temptations felt by the therapist? We also have unfulfilled needs. Our hormones do not differentiate which members of the opposite sex are off limits. So we try to ignore our own needs for intimacy, for sexual contact, for friendship with clients. Many of our clients not only look good to us but feel good to know. They are people not unlike ourselves—motivated to grow. They have been dedicated learners. Some have worked very hard to turn themselves into our Pygmalions. They can express feelings fluently, use the language and terms we favor. They have been completely open, sharing, and honest with us. They have disclosed their histories, fantasies, dreams, and desires. And for this dedicated effort, we like many of them a lot.

The consequences of acting on our erotic impulses are obvious. We not only lose our objectivity but jeopardize the trust and therapeutic work that have been accomplished. Sexual contact with clients or ex-clients is usually an abuse of trust and power and is always self-indulgent and antitherapeutic. Many of the victims of "therapeutic incest" experience lowered self-esteem; sexual dysfunctions; feelings of exploitation; anger, and betrayal; and a feeling of mistrust toward other helping professionals that makes them reluctant to seek treatment for their now-compounded problems (Zelen, 1985). We know all of this. And that is why we work so hard to restrain our natural (and unnatural) desires.

Other aspects of the therapeutic relationship are less clearly delineated. If Holroyd and Brodsky (1977) report that 6 percent of the therapists they surveyed admitted to having had sexual intercourse with clients and we assume that such activity is probably more pervasive than reported, what percentage of practicing therapists have had other forms of erotic contact with clients? Since the increasingly firm stand on the dangers of sexual involvement was taken by professional organizations, the reported incidence has been declining (Pope & Vasquez, 1991), perhaps due to better training or, more cynically, because of less honesty on the part of respondents.

And then there are gray areas in the restraint of intimacy. Some practitioners restrict their therapeutic activities to their offices, whereas others work wonders in the outside world. The difficulty of maintaining intimacy boundaries increases during field trips, sessions conducted in restaurants, at picnic tables, or on bike rides. The temptation to become involved with clients beyond appropriate limits is more severe. The therapist must exercise incredible self-monitoring, self-control, self-deprivation. The pressure builds.

Restraint

The cumulative pressures from maintaining prolonged one-way intimacy are hardship enough for a professional who also requires liberal doses of approval and hugging. The tension is compounded by other ways a therapist exhibits restraint. From graduate school onward we are told what things we must not do during sessions with clients. Most of all, we are warned not to do too much; it is the client's responsibility to do the work, choose the content, pace the progress, develop insight, and change behavior. Embedded in the admonishment to avoid doing too much to rescue the client is an unwieldy list of more specific negative imperatives.

- Do not express personal opinions.
- Do not take sides.
- Do not be too passive.
- Do not be too directive.
- Do not moralize or let personal values show.
- Do not let your attention wander.
- Do not let clients know how you really feel about them.
- Do not have a vested interest in the direction the client chooses.
- Do not meet your own needs during sessions.
- Do not ask close-ended questions.
- Do not share too much of yourself.
- Do not hide behind a professional mask.
- Be honest, but do not say everything you are thinking.
- Use restraint, but do not act mechanically.
- Be genuine, but do not be too transparent.

Depending on one's training, of course, this personal list of precautions will vary. There is usually a theme of "stifle yourself" juxtaposed with encouragement to be authentic.

We know what happens to children who deliberately withhold their true feelings, repress their unsatisfied needs: they become neurotic, well-disciplined adults. We know what happens to children in a double-bind family where they get mixed messages: they become confused or even crazy. What happens to therapists who experience these same things?

Self-deprivation comes with the territory. We are trained and paid well to put others' welfare before our own. We are disciplined to diffuse our own desires. "By dispassionately acknowledging our personal needs, we lessen their grip on our actions. More and more we simply observe rather than identify with our motives. It's not so much that we are trying to push them away; denial buys us no peace. Rather, we are loosening our attachment to our motives by stepping behind them" (Ram Dass & Gorman, 1985, p. 193).

In our drive to be therapeutic, we harness self-centered urges. Yet it is hard to tread water with someone on our back without drowning. We can only give so much without needing support in return. And just when we have achieved that miracle of therapeutic love, when we feel comfortable and safe, when we even look forward to the meetings with clients we have grown attached to, it is time to say good-bye.

Termination anxiety in the therapist is elicited by several factors enumerated by Martin and Schurtman (1985). Unresolved separation and fears of abandonment can be rekindled as a profound sense of loss. These feelings are further complicated by the therapist's natural reactions to the client's ambivalence over termination. The clinician may feel guilt, failure, disappointment, sadness, pride, apprehension, hope, jealousy, and/or relief—all at once. And there is the constant cycle of growing immensely fond of people and then turning them loose.

As the Little Prince tamed the fox through the observation of proper rites and regularly scheduled meetings and became responsible for him, so do we feel love and obligation toward the people whose hearts and intellects we first tame and then set free. "You become responsible, forever, for what you have tamed" (de Saint-Exupéry, 1943, p. 88).

Narcissism

Restraining our egos is a challenge many of us will never quite meet. What with our diplomas, titles, and carefully appointed chambers, it is hard for us not to take ourselves seriously. Such self-centered preoccupation with the image we project to the world is hazardous to our mental health. We become disembodied selves, separated from our feelings and from those of the people we try to help.

In Lowen's (1983) treatise on narcissism he describes a pervasive disease of our time that strikes therapists as well as their clients. A lack of feeling, the need to project an image, the desire to help others in order to exercise power, and arrogance are all familiar symptoms. Lowen further describes the phallic-narcissistic personality, portraying himself and many colleagues in a mold of exaggerated confidence, energy, dignity, and superiority. We *do* act as though we know what is going on most of the time.

From their study of narcissism in therapists, Herron and

Rouslin (1984) and Welt and Herron (1990) conclude that this obsessional defense has its roots in our need for control. The desire to help is masked by self-interest, by power, by competition, by seeking to win approval, and by spoors. Yes, spoors — leaving our tracks behind.

Honestly consider for a moment the real kick you get out of being a therapist — besides the benefits mentioned in the previous chapter. I suspect that deep within my own heart is the desperate need to influence others. I am afraid of dying and, worse, of being forgotten. I feel as though I am in the process of immortalizing myself with every disciple who goes out into the world with a part of me inside him or her. It is as if I can cheat death if only I can keep a part of me alive. Does this motive affect what I do in my sessions? Naturally. Does this grandiose self-involvement limit the quality of my work? Of course. Do I feel impaired in my capacity for empathy because of this narcissism? Unfortunately, yes. But I stay safe. "Empathy means that at a level beyond the therapist's control, the patient is influencing him or her, not intellectually but emotionally. This implies, then, that the therapist is vulnerable, subject to experiencing any feelings, intense feelings, uncomfortable feelings, almost against his or her will" (Herron & Rouslin, 1984, p. 117).

To give up our narcissistic stance is to risk a deeper, more terrifying form of self-involvement: confronting the feelings we fear most. Like most obsessives, we successfully distract ourselves from those things we least wish to understand. We can avoid real intimacy even in our sacred chambers by keeping clients at a distance. We can glorify the influence we have had on clients while denying their influence on us. With casual grace we can sever a two-, three-, or four-year relationship as if we are dismissing a stray dog with a pat on the rump.

We can distance ourselves from pain by retreating deep inside our chairside manner—a few strokes of the chin, a blank stare, a delusion that we have the power to heal. Enter a woman in her mid thirties who is far from composed. Suffering oozes from her pores; even her tears have tears. She feels hopeless, despondent, deeply depressed. This is her third attempt to seek help in as many weeks. The last therapist she saw for six sessions.

> *"What did he say?"*
>
> *"I don't know."*
>
> *"You don't remember?"*
>
> *"I remember quite well. He didn't say anything."*
>
> *"He said nothing?"*
>
> *"No."*
>
> *"What, then, did he do during the time you spent together?"*
>
> *"He took notes."*
>
> *"Uh huh."*
>
> *"He said thank you when I paid him at the end."*
>
> *"Why did you go back if you didn't feel he helped you?"*
>
> *"He seemed so important. He came highly recommended. And he seemed so awfully busy. He*

*had to arrange things to fit me into his schedule,
and several times he was interrupted by calls from
people who needed him. I thought maybe if I
waited long enough he might notice me. But he
only seemed to notice himself. It's like he looked
right through me, as if I wasn't there. I felt like a
bug he was inspecting. All he did was take notes.
Even when I broke down sobbing he just looked at
me across his desk and kept writing in his pad."*

The woman stopped abruptly, peeked out from behind
her anguish. I asked her if she would give me a chance to
help her. She said she was tired of seeing therapists but she
would think about it and let me know. She drove straight
home, drew a bath, swallowed twelve antidepressants,
drank a pint of bourbon, and slit both her wrists. She died
from the chronic indifference and narcissism of the therapists who refused to see her as a human being.

There is a danger in using anecdotal material such as
this to support assumptions about therapist characteristics
and experiences. We all know individuals in our profession
who believe themselves to be godlings and demand homage
from their disciples. We also are familiar with popular
accounts of our brethren by authors such as Miller (1981)
and Lowen (1983), who portray us as a cruelly grandiose,
narcissistic lot. "The field of psychotherapy inevitably at-
tracts people with god complexes, and it is custom designed
to exacerbate the condition when it exists" (Maeder, 1989,
p. 45). Nevertheless, in a study designed to test the notion

that therapists are more narcissistic than others, Clark
(1991) found no evidence for this idea. Although this investigation was based on a very small sample, it does remind us
to be careful of exaggerating a problem that, although it
may not be widespread, is at least something that we should
monitor in ourselves. Therapists in our society are, after all,
treated *as if* we have special powers that allow us to see inside
people's hearts and souls, predict the future, and heal suffering. It is indeed difficult for us not to come to believe in our
specialness.

Fatigue

In an article on his life-style, one prominent therapist describes a typical day as being so rigidly scheduled from 7:00
A.M. to 2:00 A.M. the following morning that each fifteen-
minute segment of time is meticulously accounted for. Sessions are run back to back without a break. Meals are inhaled
between administrative, lecturing, writing, and consulting
chores, and even conversations must be scheduled in advance (Ellis, 1983). Although he defends this inhumane
regimen as an "affair of the heart," it could more accurately
be described as a case of "neurotic workaholism" that is part
of a maladaptive vicious circle (Penzer, 1984).

Time pressures head the list of therapist stressors (Nash,
Norcross, & Prochaska, 1984). There are never enough hours
to see all the people we need to see, return phone calls,
attend meetings, complete paperwork, do outreach, keep
up with the literature, eat, sleep, and have a life outside of

the office. We often run behind schedule. There are often people waiting, yet there is always room for just one more client.

Once the door closes and we immerse ourselves in a session, one would think the narrowed focus on a single life and task would provide some relief from the exhausting pace. With distractions and intrusions kept at bay, the rhythm of the day slowed down to that of the client's heartbeat, we can feel our profound weariness. It is so hard to sit still. Our knees ache; our eyes burn. We experience greater risks of lower back pain and circulatory and metabolic disorders than the population at large (Bellack & Faithorn, 1981). After the eighth, ninth, tenth, or eleventh session in a row there is little left beyond an empty shell.

We get so tired of sitting, of listening, of talking, of thinking. This fatigue comes upon us from a number of sources described by English (1972): when a therapist takes on too much work out of greed to make more money, or out of pride to test one's limits, or out of habit because it is the path of least resistance, or out of control to protect one's territory, or out of fear of confronting the rest of one's life, emotional and physical tiredness eventually will ensue. "It is, of course, a well known fact that one of the principal causes of a psychotherapist's vulnerability to fatigue is his/her own unresolved emotional problems. They tend to distort one's perception of the patient and his or her problems, to over-identify with the patient, and to use the patient for one's own purposes. These misperceptions and misidentifications often result in entanglements with patients, leading to distress and failure, if not to flight and mental illness, including suicide" (Dai, 1979, p. 27).

Griswell (1979, pp. 50–51) notices the times he feels weary are those when he is blocking some other feeling: "In one session with a client where tiredness tugged at my sleeve, I found a resentment I had pushed aside about his call at the last minute to cancel our previous session. In another, I looked under the feelings of tiredness and got in touch with some sexual feelings I wasn't acknowledging to myself. With another the feelings were ones of danger and the client volunteered that she was feeling self-destructive and not telling me."

Much of the time we urge clients to avoid the excesses of overwork. We caution moderation to reduce stress, fatigue, and mental exhaustion. We teach people to better appreciate their present moments, to live a tranquil existence. We do all of this while exhibiting the same symptoms of the workaholic.

On a more serious note, we show symptoms of overwork when we skip meals or refuse to decline work when we are already overloaded. We neglect family, friends, and, most of all, ourselves. There is so little time to be alone, to think, to feel, to do nothing. Some of us are reluctant to take more than a few days off work because we fear losing income or losing power in the organizational structure. It doesn't take others very long to realize we are replaceable—even if we nurture the illusion that we must do everything ourselves because nobody else could do as good a job.

When we are not working we mull over our cases. We

consider the direction our clients will head next, the things we did that we wish we had not done, and our plans for the following week. At odd moments we wonder how clients are getting along. Why did they never return? What did we do to chase them away? These people populate our world. We see them more frequently than we see most of our friends. No matter how much we work to preserve our professional detachment, no matter how hard we discipline ourselves to push them out of our minds when they walk out the door, we still carry them around inside of us. How could these people not be significant in our lives and loom in our minds when we spend week after week after week discussing the sacred details of their lives?

I feel exhausted; my energy is depleted just thinking about the burdens we routinely carry. It is strange to think we work so hard while sitting still. Maybe it is because we must remain immobile and attentive that the job is so tiring. If only we could separate ourselves from the chair. If only our existence outside the chair could be as meaningful as the time we spend enveloped within it.

The Workaholic Therapist

A common precursor to full-fledged burnout is a condition that we are often asked to treat in others—the workaholic syndrome. This occurs when a person has become addicted to a job, is obsessed with being productive, and feels an internal drive to work long hours that exceed the expectations of one's colleagues (Maslach, 1986). Because therapists who are addicted to their work (and I must honestly number myself among this group) gain tremendous satisfaction and happiness from what they are doing, their behavior is usually more of a problem for others than for themselves, especially if they have expectations that colleagues should be more like them.

Unless sufficient care is taken, the therapist's family life will suffer, and eventually symptoms of burnout may develop from chronic stress. Just as we would suggest for clients presenting this condition (who presumably are coming in because they or their families acknowledge that there is indeed a problem), we must confront and deal with issues from the past.

The first and most important predictor of successful life-style change involves the therapist's *wanting* to get off the treadmill. Tony has no interest in doing so. He conducts thirty individual and family sessions during the week, runs two groups on Saturdays, and functions as an administrator of his clinic for another twenty hours per week. He is making a lot of money but claims he has no time to spend it. Does he like this kind of life?

"I don't know. I don't really think about it much. Yeah, I guess I do. Or I wouldn't keep doing it, would I?"

"Can you really be all that helpful to your clients seeing so many back to back?"

"Well, they keep coming back, don't they?"

Dierdre, on the other hand, fully acknowledges she is out of control. It started after her divorce with the determination that she would show her ex-husband, her children, her parents—she would show the world that she could make it just fine on her own. She supplemented her work in a public agency with a part-time practice that blossomed to the point where she had more clients than hours in the day. Yet she found it hard to turn down a referral or set limits on her time. She was reveling in her financial and professional success but mourned the loss of not seeing her children grow up. They had become used to her never being around.

Like so many of our startling revelations, Dierdre's came from seeing herself in a client—the same defenses, the identical excuses for not changing: "Sure, I need to cut back. And I will someday. For now, though, I'll see if I can go just a little longer."

Cutting back for Dierdre meant giving up some of her financial perks. It meant she had to face her dismal social life. It meant she had to relearn how to parent her own children. Most of all, curtailing her workaholic style meant that she had to create a life for herself, an identity for herself other than as a therapist.

Futility

The business of therapy not only is draining but sometimes leads to feelings of despondency. One psychiatrist describes how the futility of the work setting precipitated a major depressive episode, one that landed him in the hospital.

"There was a gulf between my aspirations (often unrealistic) and the aspirations for their fulfillment. . . . I considered that I was in the midst of unimaginative, slipshod psychiatry and tortured myself because I could not put it right" (Wakeling, 1985, p. 13).

It is this feeling of impotence — that no matter what you do, or how well you do it, your efforts are wasted — that leads the therapist to first lose innocence, then compassion, and finally her sense of identity as a genuine helper. In a collection of essays written by nineteen therapists who had experienced major depression, Rippere and Williams (1985) noted that three-quarters of them were able to recover fully and return to work. Most of the previously disabled therapists resolved that they would do things differently and carry more realistic expectations of what was within their capacity.

In spite of our best efforts to be helpful, in spite of the client's real desire to cooperate, not all the people we work with get better; some get worse. Oh, we can delude ourselves with excuses such as (1) "The client is really changing but won't admit it," (2) "This is part of the resistance/ transference/ defenses," (3) "You have to get worse before you can get better," (4) "It just takes time, lots of time," (5) "You win a few; you lose a few." But it hurts when we fail our clients, and we do take it personally.

Perhaps *fail* is too strong a word. Still, there are times when, after years of treatment, the only apparent change a client experiences is a depleted bank account. Ellis (1984) claims it is rash if not downright irrational for therapists to believe they can be successful with all their clients. I am certain he is right. We understand that it is beyond our means to help everybody. Yet such realization does not protect us from the beliefs that "All my interpretations must be profound," "I must always make brilliant judgments," "My clients must appreciate my work and be grateful as hell," and "They should work as hard between sessions as I do when I'm with them" (Ellis, 1984).

These demands sound ridiculous if not impossible. Still, there is no surprise more devastating than receiving a Release of Information form from another therapist who is now working with an ex-client of ours. First anger and betrayal appear; then self-doubt sneaks up and builds to a thundering crescendo. If there is a colleague available to complain to, it is likely we will hear a comforting pronouncement: "You were so effective with that client that he is afraid to come back to you knowing he will have to change." Sure.

The truth is we are all incompetent some of the time. We just cannot get through to some people because of our deficiencies and limitations. Most of the time we never find out what really went wrong. The client stops coming and does not return calls. In some ways it feels even worse when a client keeps coming but will not let you get through to her; she feels strong enough and safe enough to continue therapy without the fear of having to change. It is no consolation to remind ourselves we get paid whether the client appears to change or not. We still have to deal with that stony, determined face. We still have to put up with the games, defensive reactions, and stubborn resistance and not take it personally.

There are those clients who will come forever: the passive, dependent personalities who need someone to dish out approval; the narcissistic people who need an audience; the borderline clients who, when they are not bouncing off the ceiling, need someone they can pay to abuse. It seems futile to work with these people because they will barely improve and will rarely be cured. We measure progress among the severely disturbed population in terms that are less than spectacular. We have the audacity to believe we can change the tide of a person's genetic structure, a family's rigid hierarchy, or stable personality traits that have been in place since birth. It is a miracle that we ever make a difference in these clients' lives. And it is not unusual for us to encounter a force greater than we are capable of counteracting.

It seems futile to try to convince a seventeen-year-old that we can offer him an antidote to his lust for excitement that can compete with marijuana. It is similarly hopeless to try to lure an alcoholic away from bourbon with the promise of greener pastures. It is futile to try to help an enraged adolescent when his parents sabotage treatment. When an individual jumps right back into his peer group after leaving our office, it is unrealistic to think we can alter his values. We experience futility when we attempt to cure anybody of anything. Nobody wants what we are selling until they find they have no other choice. And even then they will settle for cosmetic changes if they can just buy some time. We can give them what they want—a little relief—but we know that is futile, too.

Isolation

Therapy exists to provide a safe and private haven for people to resolve their underlying problems. Without a guarantee that communications will be held in strictest confidence, it is unlikely that any effective helping can be accomplished. To protect the client's right to privacy, secrecy, and dignity, we swear allegiance to our profession's code of conduct with regard to privileged communication. If we do nothing else in treatment, our primary obligation is to respect and protect the confidentiality of information received during sessions.

Naturally, clients appreciate our integrity and our sense of honor. For us it is second nature after years of training. We would no sooner commit an indiscretion that might compromise a client's safety than we would neglect to guard our own shameful secrets. When talking about our work in any context — with colleagues, client families, friends, and even spouses — we routinely monitor what we say so that client identities are disguised and their secrets protected. This shield serves our clients well, as presumably our prudence protects their desire for privacy. However, like all barriers, it not only prevents things from getting out, it also ensures that other things do not get in.

One of the most meaningful, interesting, and fulfilling parts of a therapist's life is the time spent with clients. At times we may be practically bursting at the seams to tell friends about some prominent citizen we are working with. And yet we can tell no one about the people we work with or about the details of what we do.

If we run into a client at a social gathering, etiquette requires us to fade into the background unless the client chooses to recognize us. If a client's name comes up in conversation, we must pretend indifference so as not to give away our involvement. It is as if we were conducting secret affairs with fifty people simultaneously! We even arrange our schedules and offices so clients do not accidentally meet one another. All of this results in a kind of sanctuary for the people we help and a kind of prison for ourselves.

Guy (1987) describes the isolation of our work as all-encompassing. Physically, we are separated from the outside world, ensconced in a soundproof chamber. We do not answer the phone, open the door, or otherwise tolerate interruptions during sessions; in the intervals in between, we are so busy doing paperwork or going to the bathroom that there is little time for interaction with anyone. Visitors rarely stop by because we are continually unavailable or "in session." It is as if when we are "in session" we cease to exist in the outside world.

What are the effects of this compartmentalized isolation? Maybe it contributes to therapists' feeling of specialness and sainthood: we suffer in silence so that others may be released from pain. We also may become secretive, mysterious, aloof, and evasive when we are not at work, while we continue to struggle to be authentic, transparent, and genuine with clients. We retreat inside ourselves for comfort and pat ourselves on the back for being so professional. Actually we feel like martyrs.

All over the city there are restaurants and bars we cannot feel comfortable visiting because clients or ex-clients work there. At parties we have to monitor closely how much we drink, knowing that losing control would sully our reputation. Neighbors watch our children for signs of emotional disturbance so they can substantiate the myth of the crazy shrink down the block. People constantly ask for advice on what to do about their jobs. Others feel intimidated by their own perception of therapists as mind readers. They will not get too close for fear we will disrobe their insecurities with a casual glance. "Oh you're a therapist. I suppose I should be careful around you. (Giggle)."

So we live on display in glass houses. If clients or prospective clients research our reputations in the community, we hope they will discover we are not only competent professionals but nice people. Because we are being watched, we stay in line and cultivate a consistent image. We watch, listen, speak when we are spoken to, and keep our mouths shut.

Conflict

Police officers do not like to break up domestic fights for two reasons. First, people in the throes of conflict can be irrational and violent toward anyone in their proximity. Second, it is painful and uncomfortable to be around people who are making complete asses of themselves. Any therapist who does marital and family work gets used to the role of participant-observer in human squabbles. Initially, we make it safe for people to feel at home and to be themselves. Then we give them permission to say what is on their minds, what is really bothering them. We may even aggravate matters a bit by provoking clients to say what they feel and respond to what has been said. We tell them conflict is constructive; then we sit back, cross our arms, and duck a lot. Even if such activities eventually prove helpful for the client, nobody can convince me that the therapist does not suffer.

Some therapists grew up in homes in which verbal abuse and active conflict were common, while others never experienced such fireworks. For those who watched their parents fight, it can be awfully uncomfortable being part of other parents' arguments—no matter how therapeutic we believe it is. For those therapists who lived in relative tranquility as children (or at least where fighting was not a spectacle), it is just as unnerving to observe people acting out their anger and resentments in passionate tirades. And it is even more difficult when they turn on us.

There is nothing worse than a client who decides he has been betrayed by his therapist. A client can turn on his therapist for a variety of irrational or justifiable reasons: as a distraction, as punishment, or just as a habit of abusing "the help." We can tell ourselves again and again, "This is not personal. This is not. . ." Yet it still hurts. At best, several difficult sessions must be devoted to working through the anger or transference. At worst, there is the threat of malpractice suits or harassment. Fisher (1985) examines the frequency with which therapists are harassed by unfounded nuisance suits that leave eternal scars. We help a dependent wife to gain her emotional freedom. She decides to divorce her husband and lives happily ever after. The husband is an attorney, and he is left feeling very miserable. Naturally, he blames the therapist for his problems, and he starts legal proceedings as a way to get even. He calls the licensing board and lodges an exaggerated complaint: "This guy brainwashed my wife. He led her astray, convinced her to divorce me. I think he slept with her, too. I hear he does that sort of thing a lot." A year-long investigation eventually will bring out the truth, but not before the therapist has had to fight for his reputation, defend himself to his peers, and survive the mental anguish of harassment.

We hear horror stories about or know of colleagues who are actually stalked by ex-clients or their families. They must change their phone numbers, watch over their shoulders, sometimes even relocate their homes. One psychiatrist had been working with a disturbed young woman for a very short time when her estranged husband began to harass him by repeatedly showing up at his doorstep. Even after the psychiatrist moved, he was still tracked down, his privacy invaded, and his life threatened. Another counselor became too informal and friendly with a hysterical client and paid for his mistake dearly. After two years of attempting to discourage the client's professions of love, numerous court orders and phone number changes, and complete silence on the part of the counselor, he still receives six to eight messages per day on his answering machine. Maybe it is not all that surprising that such incidences occur considering that our clients and their families frequently suffer from mental disturbances. By definition, our clients are emotionally immature and behaviorally inept. How can we hope to be around such conflict without some of it rubbing off on us?

What happens to a therapist who constantly watches

other people screaming and arguing? He develops a callous and cavalier attitude, and grows desensitized to emotional trauma. Or he becomes one of the walking wounded with a case of battle fatigue. Whenever voices reach a certain decibel level, he flinches involuntarily. Whatever the case, a therapist's tolerance for witnessing conflict and remaining in control of the situation changes — quantitatively or qualitatively. If we have to play King Solomon on the job we may not feel like doing so at home. Let someone else make the decisions and run the show.

I personally have great difficulty dealing with people who are mad at me, even when I have done nothing wrong. But I have to deal with them anyway. A client owed me money for two years. I wrote a firm letter requesting payment immediately. In return I received a message on my answering machine that was loud, angry, incoherent. I guessed she had had a setback and would not be paying her bill. A mother called me every week to complain about what a lousy job I was doing with her son (he was trying to break away from his mother). Whenever I suggested she take her son elsewhere, she became even more irate. She would do no such thing. I started this mess so I had to clean it up. "Yes, Mrs. X. Thank you for calling." Another client indignantly canceled all further appointments after learning that we had a mutual acquaintance. I called to refer her to another therapist, and she acted as if it were part of a conspiracy. A marital case became a divorce case, and they acted as though it were my fault. An insurance company decided not to reimburse a client; again, it was my fault. And, of course, whenever clients do not get better fast enough it is always our fault.

No matter how good we are, no matter how well trained and supervised, no matter how experienced we become, inevitably we must confront the limits of our abilities and admit that we cannot help everyone. Some clients do not want to be helped; others are not ready to change; still others move at a pace far slower than we can tolerate.

These negative outcomes are threatening to us and to our sense of potency, so much so that we have a number of ways we keep failure at a distance (Kottler & Blau, 1989).

- *Define failure as success*: "The reason he did not return after the first session is that he was cured."
- *Subscribe to minimal expectations*: "As long as she keeps coming back, she must be getting something out of therapy."
- *Pretend you are succeeding*: "He is really improving, he just won't admit it."
- *Blame factors outside your control*: "How can I make much of a difference when this client has such severe disturbances?"
- *Insist the client is not ready to change*: "My job is simply to wait until the client decides to take charge of his or her life."

Being bright, perceptive, and psychologically sophisticated folks, if we are going to find excuses to explain negative outcomes, they will be very good ones. Certainly these explanations do have merit.

Methods of warding off the confrontation with failure, and of subsequent stress reduction, do not take into consideration what many practitioners believe — that it is the client who succeeds or fails, not the therapist. Nevertheless, whether we admit it or not, we cannot help but be affected by a client who is deteriorating before our eyes and for whom there is nothing we can do to stop the downward slide. Approximately one-fifth of the negative endings in therapy leave the clinician feeling troubled indefinitely, unable to resolve the conflict internally (Elkind, 1992).

Money

Therapy is practiced differently in various settings. The clinical approach chosen, the length of treatment, and the methodologies employed will depend, to a large extent, on economic realities. In a community mental health center with a two-week waiting list and funding contingent on the number of new patients enrolled, it is unlikely that psychoanalytic treatment will be all that popular. And in private practice, where a therapist's livelihood depends on being able to consistently sell one's time by the hour, it is unusual to find someone practicing short-term behavioral therapy interventions. A therapist with a large turnover might require more than four hundred new referrals every year just to survive, whereas another clinician could get by quite comfortably with ten or twelve.

We belong to a profession whose members cannot decide whether they are scientists or philosophers, technicians or artists. We cannot agree on whether therapists should be trained in schools of medicine, education, liberal arts, or social work. We cannot agree on whether therapy takes a short time or a long time, whether it ought to focus on the past or the present, whether the therapist or the client should define the problem we are to work on, or even whether the therapist should talk a lot or a little. And, perhaps more importantly, we cannot decide whether therapy is essentially a profession or a business. Frank (1979) candidly admits that once upon a time he did therapy to help people but now he does it for money. Whereas once helping people was fun, now it is work. And he is not ashamed to admit that a part of every therapy hour is spent calculating how much he earned while listening to someone tell his or her story.

Therapists have a tangled relationship with money, creating guilt and conflict in our lives (Herron & Welt, 1992). In her article on the "last taboo" of our field, Mellan (1992) describes a few of the different ways in which practitioners deal with their ambivalence about charging money for a helping relationship. Some identify with the role of "monk," in which they believe that having too much money will corrupt them; they experience a tremendous amount of anxiety and conflict over the business aspects of their work. Others feel like prostitutes—they are providing intimacy to strangers for a fee. And quite a number of practitioners in private practice feel guilty about being paid a lot of money to do work that they love.

When we splice into the picture feelings prevalent among clinicians that they are not really doing much in their work anyway, that they are frauds who are just paid to listen, guilt can lead to a vicious cycle. Based on the feeling that because the money has not really been earned, it is best to get rid of it as quickly as possible, our life-style can become one of consumerism—of work, spend, work, spend (Schor, 1992). One therapist of my acquaintance was incredibly busy, seeing fifty to sixty clients per week and making more money than any reasonable person could hope to spend. With no leisure time to shop in person, she shopped by phone between sessions, eventually ordering so much catalogue merchandise that she worked herself into unrecoverable debt.

To complicate money matters further, even while we are dealing with the guilt of feeling overpaid for doing so little, marveling at the salary we are paid to do what we most love, we struggle with the corresponding feeling that there is not enough money in the world to compensate us for the tedium and abuse we must put up with. Nobody works as hard as we do mediating battles between family members, dealing with surly adolescents who nobody else can handle, and seeing people in anguish and suffering.

The vicious cycle of a consumer-oriented life-style was played out in my own life. I was working *so* hard, helping so many people, that I wanted to reward myself. Maybe a new car would be fun. It would cost only a few hundred dollars a month, and I would need to add just one more client to my caseload to pay for it. But then I found myself working even harder to pay the bills. I needed an even bigger reward.

Eventually, money issues got the best of me. I could not reconcile doing this kind of work to help people with being paid directly by them for the privilege. I was amazed by colleagues who had no compunctions about this dilemma; some even demanded payment before the sessions began. I noticed, as my delinquent accounts rose, how angry I felt at my clients for not paying promptly. The financial stresses and strains of private practice took their toll. I was no longer a therapist: I felt like a businessman. Abruptly, I quit and went back into public service, where I had begun my career. For two years I saw clients on the side for free until I could rekindle my joy for therapeutic work. Only very gradually did I begin to feel comfortable charging a fee once again, and then only on a limited basis.

Each of us has a personal relationship with money, a circumstance that creates additional hardships in our work. We see couples who argue about money or who will not talk about the subject at all. We see disadvantaged clients who have no money, sparking guilt that we have too much. We see wealthy individuals who fritter away their funds in a search for fulfillment. Envy, resentment, and pity get in the way of our compassion. And when it comes to managing our own resources, each of us has issues that impinge on our work and can muddle things quite a bit.

Once upon a time, the practice of therapy, like that of medicine or law, was a calling. It was less a job or a career than it was a commitment to helping. There was passion and single-minded devotion to a simpler world with simpler ideals. Then the baby boomers hit the job market, and the market tightened up. The image of the therapist was transformed from that of a kindly country doctor dispensing advice to that of a consummate professional with computer and psychometric support. Legislators began regulating the field. Professional organizations mandated appropriate conduct. Insurance companies got into the act, followed by health maintenance organizations and preferred provider plans. Now competition for customers is the name of the game for many therapists and mental health organizations.

Clinicians are caught between images of themselves as missionaries and behavior that is more characteristic of manufacturers' representatives. We feel angry about being unappreciated and underpaid. Sometimes it seems that no amount of money could fairly compensate us for the aggravation, intensity, emotional turmoil, conflict, and frustration. Other times we feel guilty about being overpaid for doing nothing. In exchange for spending forty-five minutes listening to someone talk and then telling them what we think about what they said, we receive enough money to buy ten books or a whole night on vacation. It is absurd. It would almost seem that even with the hardships of being a therapist, we have a great thing going. If only we did not encounter those clients who push us to the brink of our own madness.

chapter 5

PATIENTS WHO TEST
OUR PATIENCE

$\int$ome of the perils a therapist encounters are an implicit part of the job. Just as a construction worker would hardly complain about the heights at which he must work and a soldier would not be surprised to find people shooting at him during a war, a therapist accepts the dangers of getting close to people for a living. The difficulty is in contending with some of those people.

That clinicians have strong preferences concerning whom they prefer to work with is well known. Most everyone prefers clients who are bright, eager, verbal, perceptive, affluent, and attractive. These clients not only grow quickly, but they can be patient, polite, and grateful, and they pay their bills promptly. Therapists may express preferences based on (1) the similarity to previous cases that have worked out well; (2) the probability of dealing with issues that are not personally threatening; (3) the challenge the case presents to learn something new; (4) whether the client can make a day versus an evening appointment; (5) what insurance benefits the client has; (6) whether the case falls within their spectrum of expertise; and (7) the relative likelihood that the client will be difficult to deal with. It is the last point that will be the subject of this chapter.

Countertransference

Perhaps the most thoroughly discussed hazard of therapeutic work is the classical countertransference reactions to problem clients. The term countertransference is used in several different ways — as a reference to all the feelings a therapist has toward a client, as the therapist's reactions to a client's transference, or as the therapist's own transference feelings toward a client. In each case there is the likelihood of distortion that can lead to treatment difficulties as well as the possibility that such feelings can have beneficial or detrimental effects (Singer, Sincoff, & Kolligian, 1989). Any interpretation that is offered contains a statement not only about the client but also about the therapist. Any clinical decision to choose one course of action over another is based on more than detached analysis of what is best for the client; it also represents the subjective inner world, conscious and unconscious, of the practitioner.

Manifestations in the Therapeutic Relationship

The manifestations of this therapist distortion — overidentification and overinvolvement — may take a number of different forms. Several writers (Palmer, 1980; Kottler, 1992a; Elkind, 1992; Corey & Corey, 1993) describe the symptoms that are often elicited in therapists by difficult clients.

- The arousal of guilt from unresolved personal struggles that parallel those impulses and emotions of the client
- Impaired empathy in which the therapist finds it difficult to feel loving and respectful toward the client
- Inaccurate interpretations of the client's feelings due to the therapist's identification and projection
- Therapist feelings of being generally blocked, helpless, and frustrated with a particular client
- Evidence of boredom or impatience in the therapist's inner world during work with a client
- Unusual memory lapses regarding the details of a case
- Mutual acting out in which the client begins living out the therapist's values and the therapist begins acting out the client's pathology
- A tendency to speak about a client in derogatory terms
- An awareness that you are working harder than the client

Countertransference was first uncovered by Freud in his relationships with patients (such as Dora) and colleagues (such as Fleiss and Jung). In a letter to his friend Ferenczi during a period of conflict he revealed that he was not the psychoanalytic superman that Ferenczi imagined him to be, nor had he overcome countertransference (Freud, 1955). He would develop these ideas in a paper published a few years later in which he stated that the therapist's personal feelings toward the client are both the greatest tool in treatment and the greatest obstacle (Freud, 1912). This belief was later echoed in greater detail by some neo-Freudians who thought countertransference feelings were not simply undesirable complications in the therapeutic process but real assets in the promotion of a true human encounter. Such psychodynamic theorists as Frieda Fromm-Reichmann, Franz Alexander, and Therese Benedek felt that although the analyst's personal reactions to patients could be seriously disturbing to both parties, the dangers were minimal if the analyst had undergone intensive treatment and supervision in his own analysis (Alexander & Selesnick, 1966).

There have been many refinements in therapeutic technique since Freud's day, yet clinicians still struggle with their feelings, distortions, unconscious reactions, unresolved conflicts, misperceptions, antagonism, and subjective experiences in relation to certain clients. Watkins (1985) classified countertransference responses into several broad themes that encompass oversolicitous attitudes and overprotectiveness in a parental role as well as tendencies to try to win the client's approval through benign friendliness that jeopardizes therapeutic distance. Quite opposite reactions are also elicited in us when we become punitive and aloof in response to a client's demands and dependency. In extreme cases, overt hostility and verbal abuse arise in a therapist to distance himself from the client's pathology.

The obvious point is that we are hardly the same with all our clients. A brief glimpse at the appointment book reminds us of those people we eagerly await and those we dread. We are friendlier with some clients than with others. Some clients are greeted cordially with an open smile and an offer of a beverage, while others are coolly directed to their places with a reminder of their delinquent bills.

A shallow, vulnerable, anxious, and demanding client shows up for an initial interview. She has a variety of psychosomatic complaints and reports she has seen a score of previous therapists who have treated her with Valium, Triavil, Dilantin, and Thorazine but with little therapy because she fires her doctors before they can reject her. One psychiatrist describes his intense hostility and disdain toward this client, triggered by his aversion to the way she mistreated her husband and child (Weiner, 1982, p. 78).

> *The problem that I, as the therapist, initially failed to identify was easy to see in retrospect as I examined my conscious reaction to this woman. I had felt angry with her, was critical of her, and wanted as little as possible to do with her, hardly an attitude that would stimulate rapport. She probably was aware of my attitude during our first session, but, not being entirely certain, brought to my attention my failure to suggest a second appointment. I had wanted to dismiss her with an explanation of her symptoms and a suggestion about medication. She was interested in treatment, but I found it impossible to hear that. To me, her voice had been harsh and grating, her attitude demanding, and her interests deploringly selfish.*

Some theorists, such as Weisman (1973) and Cerney (1985), consider intense therapist reactions, when recognized, to be crucial in diagnosing how others probably respond to the client. And it is much easier now to admit to countertransference reactions. There is no longer any shame associated with the confession that we have strong emotional reactions—both positive and negative—toward our clients.

Some Therapist Fantasies

When reactive feelings are ignored, denied, distorted, and projected, both the client's treatment and the therapist's mental health suffer. Herron and Rouslin (1984) urge clinicians to examine their fantasies with clients as a clue to how countertransference may be operating. Whether these fantasies are primarily rescue oriented, sexual in content, or expressive in rage, frustration, and anger, most therapists entertain fantasies and daydream about many of their clients. The following descriptions of reactions toward clients come from a mixed group of social workers, marriage counselors, and psychologists.

> *I genuinely love a few of my patients. I mean, I love them as much as I love my sister, my best friend, or my husband. I suppose, in a way, a few of my patients have become my closest friends. I think about them during the day, and when I do, I feel warm inside. I have known this one patient for about seven years and I like her so much. I feel sad sometimes that I can only know her as her therapist*

because I would very much enjoy meeting her for lunch and telling her about my own life.

This guy I've been seeing for a few months is the president of a major corporation. He's got a tremendous amount of power and responsibility. He hires and fires people at whim, and he's let me know that I'm under his scrutiny as well. I think about how great it would be if I help this guy, that maybe he would invite me into his company to work with his people. He's got offices all over the world and I think about traveling from Bangkok to Rio putting out fires.

I work with this one incredibly attractive woman. She has a crush on me and we both know it. She wears these outrageously revealing outfits and acts quite seductively. Naturally, I interpreted her obvious attempts to sabotage the sessions, and she has toned down quite a lot. But sometimes I feel this almost uncontrollable urge to get down on my knees and stick my head underneath her dress.

I could strangle this guy he's so whiney and complaining. He exhibits everything I despise in other people and myself: passivity, external control, helplessness, incompetence. I know he knows that I don't really like him much. But he's so used to having people not like him that my relationship

*with him seems normal. I end up feeling like he
does — helpless — because he refuses to change. As I
listen to him talk in his high-pitched monotone. I
idly wonder what creative things I could do to break
through his inhibited exterior. I picture myself slap-
ping his face or laughing at him. Then I feel such
guilt because I lose my compassion.*

*I sometimes imagine what it would be like to be
married to a few of my clients. This one guy is just a
doll, and he's trying so hard to improve himself.
He's just my type — strong but self-reflective. There
are times during the week I wonder what he's doing. I also wonder what he'd look like without his
clothes on.*

These and other fantasies represent only one narrow
aspect of the therapist's phenomenological world, and they
are certainly not typical of the way we think about our clients
all, or even most, of the time. Occasionally, however, such
fantasies give us clues to how we are personally reacting to
our clients. Only when we are willing to identify and explore
how we feel about our clients and how it affects our clinical
judgment can we ever hope to harness this energy
constructively.

Difficult Cases

Among experienced therapists there is some consensus concerning problem clients. Borderline personalities, socio-

pathic personalities, and those with personality disorders test a therapist's patience and defenses. The prognoses are poor; progress, if any, is slow; and the therapist is likely to be on the receiving end of manipulation, dramatic and painful transference, and projective identification.

A number of studies (Farber, 1983b; Colson et al. 1986; Otani, 1989) on client behaviors that are experienced by therapists as most stressful create a consistent portrait of most frequently mentioned occurrences; threats of suicide, expressions of anger, demonstrations of hostility, severe depression, abject apathy, and premature termination. Several studies (Farber & Heifetz, 1981; Deutsch, 1984; Robbins, Beck, Mueller, & Mizener, 1988; Kottler, 1992a) on client characteristics that therapists experience as most difficult and stressful to work with include the following.

- Clients with physiological disorders (strokes, closed head injuries)
- Clients with hidden agendas (workers' compensation or court referrals)
- Clients who ignore boundaries (chronic lateness or missed appointments)
- Clients who refuse responsibility ("you fix me")
- Clients who are argumentative (hostility, skepticism)
- Clients who fear intimacy (avoidant or seductive behavior)
- Clients who are incompatible (want something you cannot or will not give them)

- Clients who push the therapist's buttons (bring up his or her unresolved issues)
- Clients who are countertransference objects (remind the therapist of persons from the past)
- Clients who are impatient ("fix me quick")
- Clients who are literal and concrete (unable to access or express internal states)
- Clients who feel hopeless (actively suicidal)
- Clients with poor impulse control (offenders, substance abusers)

As therapists, we see the most perverse, bizarre, sometimes even the most evil parts of human existence. We are constantly exposed to cruelty, conflict, deception, manipulation, cynicism, mistrust, and betrayal. We see people at their absolute worst. We are privy to their most secret, hidden selves. We are the folks delegated to pick up the pieces after disappointment, divorce, or death.

There are clients we encounter whose main purpose in life seems to be making others miserable. They are schooled in the intricacies of sociopathic, narcissistic, hysterical, or borderline behavior. They know just how to get underneath our skin, and they feel most fulfilled when they succeed. All through the rage and despondency and conflict we are supposed to remain unperturbed. The sheer energy it takes to stay calm and in control in the face of such behavior is a major drain on our resources.

Borderline Clients

Masterson (1983) characterizes many clients, and especially those with borderline tendencies, as experts in searching out and exploiting the therapist's vulnerabilities. In this way the client is working just as hard to destabilize the therapist as the therapist is in trying to get to the client. Only by promoting countertransference reactions in the therapist can the client hope to buttress his own resistance and thereby avoid threats of intrapsychic conflict.

To illustrate the power of borderline clients, Kramer and Weiner (1983, p. 72) report on how therapists feel hypnotized to satisfy their disturbed client's expectations and to act out in much the same way the borderline client would: "A therapist says she had an argument with her husband one day and found herself sulking on her front step, thinking, 'I'll get him by getting a kitchen knife and scratching my wrists.' Startled, she realized that she might be 'catching' her patient's habitual responses."

All theorists who have ever written on the subject of borderline clients warn of countertransference issues being crucial to the treatment (Campbell, 1982). The therapist cannot avoid the excessive demands made on her, the dependency, aggression, and attacks that are common. All the usual subtle interventions, such as interpretations, are ineffective. We must reach into our bag of tricks and pull out something that will both help the client stay in line and protect us from abuse. Similar dynamics operate with narcissistic, passive-dependent, hysterical, and obsessive clients in that the therapist may find herself unconsciously sucked into the client's ploys and games.

A social worker had been working with an obsessive client for two long years without noticing any appreciable difference in her behavior. The client was staying the same, still ruminating merrily along, but the therapist was slowly deteriorating. He started taking the case very personally, was unresponsive to supervision in which he was cautioned to back off, and eventually dropped out of the field because he could not work through his own fears of failure. The client merely transferred to another therapist in the clinic and began slowly chipping away at his sense of potency. (Incidentally, this client had been abandoned by her father and divorced by her husband.)

Difficult Client Behaviors

A few clinicians thrive on the challenge of personality disorders. Others are remarkably patient and effective with people manifesting psychotic symptoms or with drug abusers or the intellectually impaired. But for most therapists, several patterns of client behavior are difficult to deal with.

I Got Held Up in Traffic. Resistance, in all its manifestations, is hardly the nuisance and obstruction to treatment that Freud once believed. Whether clients are overly compliant or dramatically hostile, we now understand that they are doing the very best they can to keep themselves together. We also remind ourselves constantly that missed or chronically late appointments are not part of a conspiracy to make us miserable, but rather the client's attempt to retain some control in a threatening situation. Ideally, clients will stick around long enough and therapists will exercise sufficient patience and set firm enough limits to allow the resistance to be worked through.

Noncompliance by playing with space and time arrangements in therapy is one of those things graduate students are taught to expect but nevertheless are not prepared to handle effectively. No one likes to be stood up (flashback to adolescent rejection), even if she is being paid for the idle time. Some therapists protect themselves by keeping a favorite novel sitting on the desk so if a client is "held up in traffic" or "the car broke down" or "the meeting ran over," the gap can be happily filled. But I still feel uneasy when this happens to me. And it is irritating to wait for someone, even if it is part of the treatment.

> *"Calm down. Your job is to wait for people to cure themselves."*
>
> *"That's easy for you to say. I don't like to be kept waiting. It's disrespectful and abusive."*
>
> *"Now, now. If the client knew more mature and responsible ways to express anger and resentment, he wouldn't be coming to you in the first place."*
>
> *"I know that. But I don't have to like it. In fact, it's the one part of this job I despise. I'm a punching bag who is supposed to hang suspended, bouncing back, not taking it personally when the client de-*

cides to take out on me everything he ever wanted to do to his father, mother, sister, and boot camp instructor."

"That's just the transference. You know——"

"What do you mean just? *What are you—a masochist? You* like *people to play games with your head? You enjoy being deceived, manipulated, and resisted?"*

"Yes. I probably do. Or I wouldn't be in this field. You don't mind it as much as you pretend to either."

"True. But a little cooperation would be nice occasionally. I didn't devote my life to being someone else's paid servant. I don't like always being the patient and all-forgiving one."

"Then become someone else's client."

I Want to Die. Death is the ultimate failure. It is especially tragic when someone takes his own life—not only for the victim but for those who are left behind. Family, friends, and those who tried to help experience guilt, responsibility, and regret. For any therapist who has ever lost a client through suicide there is a special sadness, a vulnerability, and a fear that it could happen again.

Suicidal clients present a challenge on multiple levels. Looming foremost in our souls is the pure emotional terror of being close to someone who is so despondent and desperate that nothingness seems like a viable option. There was a time in all our lives when we flirted with hopelessness; it was a time we would like to forget.

Second, we feel an incredible burden of responsibility in trying to help a suicidal client. There are, of course, risks of legal repercussions if things go awry. There are also moral obligations to push ourselves beyond our usual limits, to do everything within our power to be vigilant and effective. A mistake or miscalculation may have lethal consequences. We must make ourselves available day and night, on call for genuine crises or lambs crying wolf. Every threat must be taken seriously.

Third, once a risk of suicide is assessed, a different therapeutic machinery is set in motion. Records are documented meticulously. All clinical staff move cautiously, covering themselves, doing everything by the book. But it is hard to be all that therapeutic when handling a client with kid gloves. Confrontation and deep interpretations are tabled in favor of mild explorations of feeling. Until the client is once again on stable ground, most efforts are devoted to simply maintaining basic life functions while rekindling the will to survive. There is a tightrope to walk between pushing the client hard enough to get him off the fence and not pushing him over the brink. The margin for error is small, and the pressure on the therapist is profound.

A fourth challenge is in being able to leave the problems of the potentially suicidal client at work. Needless worry will not prevent a tragedy. Therapists who spend their time excessively preoccupied with clients at risk do so more for their own benefit, as a distraction and inflation of power, than for any useful purpose. We can feel important running around with pagers beeping the siren of despair. We can feel needed when we are interrupted at the most inopportune moments by a nagging voice that asks: "Did you do everything you could?"

How Do You Feel About Me? At one time or another, most clients troll for our affection. They do so as part of the transference, to get out of us what they always wanted from another, or they do so because in our role as a model we have the power to dispense approval for those actions that are desirable. Another possibility is quite simply that we are their confidants, the keepers of their secrets, and they have a natural curiosity to know how we feel about them. Although we may use evasive tactics to deny that we feel anything at all or choose to withhold such opinions as irrelevant, clients well understand the rules of the game.

With seductive clients we find our powers of restraint pushed to the limit. Some of them are determined to have their way. Klopfer (1974) outlines many reasons why seductive clients can be persistent. Conquering a therapist is the ultimate victory, proof that anyone can be corrupted. It is a way in which the client can regain control of the relationship and win power and approval. It satisfies the desire to flirt with the forbidden, and it gives the client a means to frustrate the therapist just as she has been frustrated by the therapeutic experience. It is also the best way for a client to confound the relationship, sidetrack the treatment, and prevent further therapeutic assaults.

The therapist's efforts to confront the client regarding the seductive behavior often lead to frustration. If the feelings are discussed directly and the therapist gently yet firmly rejects the overtures, the client may feel humiliated and rejected. If transference feelings are interpreted, the client may fall back on denial. Yet if the therapist attempts to back off and let things ride for a while, the seductive efforts may escalate. There is no easy solution.

One other part of this problem deserves attention: clients may behave seductively for other than sexual reasons. Often sexuality becomes confused with intimacy, especially when a man and a woman are alone together in a room. Many seductive clients do not have the slightest interest in a physical relationship but would like to establish an emotional one. This problem is just as common when the client and the therapist are of the same sex. The client feels she is giving, giving, giving and getting precious little of a personal nature in return. This perception is accurate and part of the grand design of things. The client therefore must exercise considerable ingenuity to find out what her therapist really thinks of her. Clients may measure the time it takes us to return their phone calls, how many minutes we will allow the session to run over, or the frequency of smiles as indications of our true regard.

The therapeutic relationship is a unique and asymmetrical contractual arrangement in which the therapist retains complete control to reveal about himself only what he likes. "Thus, from the therapist's standpoint, the therapeutic transaction provides intimacy and close personal familiarity without, at the same time, involving the risks entailed in revealing one's inner thoughts and feelings to one another" (Henry, Sims, & Spray, 1973, p. 219).

For people who are already insecure about where they stand in relation to others' esteem, the therapist's detachment drives them even further away. The clients who get better eventually work all of this insecurity through and become all the more autonomous because of it. But a few clients consider it their personal mission in life to get to the therapist—if not physically, then emotionally.

This Isn't Helping but I'm Coming Back. There are less obvious ways to resist treatment, such as by being overly compliant ("This is so much fun") or using the classical defenses of repression and denial ("I had a happy childhood"), but a direct challenge to our competence is the most difficult to stomach. Sometimes these resistant clients are the most diligent as far as keeping appointments, showing up on time, and at least pretending to do what they are supposed to do to get better. But they keep getting worse, and we may not know why. Oh, we have ready responses to give them.

- You'll get better when you're ready to.
- You're getting better but you just don't know it yet.

- You don't really want the responsibility of getting better.
- This is a normal part of the treatment and an indication we are heading in the right direction.
- This is really frustrating for you.

Deep down inside we are afraid to admit the naked truth: we do not know what we are doing with this client, and we cannot figure out why the client keeps coming back to remind us of our ineptitude. Certainly the key to the puzzle is what the client *does* get out of returning to the sessions without any apparent gain. Beneath the surface lies the client's hidden agenda.

For ninety consecutive sessions Brenda entered the office just as the second hand crossed the twelve. She always paid in cash, crisp twenty-dollar bills, which she insisted I count. Each week she took her place, looked up, and sneered. Her opening remark, cutting and cynical, usually sent shivers up and down my neck: "Well, as you probably expect, I'm still not feeling very well. I know I'm a fool for coming here every week, paying you my good money to listen to you pretend you care if I live or die. We both know you're in it for the bucks, but God do you look foolish sitting there acting like you know all about me. You don't know shit. When are you going to give up and give me the boot?"

Suddenly one day, just as I had dreamed it would happen, her facade came tumbling down, exposing a quivering, vulnerable human being. I honestly do not think it was because of anything specific that I did—unless you count ninety consecutive sessions of waiting for her to make the first move. She later explained that all that time she was just waiting until she felt she could trust me.

As long as these clients can keep us off balance, we will not be able to get close to them. Since they are used to functioning in antagonistic-affectionate relationships, even our disdain does not disturb them. Their goal is to keep us in line until they decide they are ready to give up the verbal combat. In the meantime it is kind of fun for them to ridicule this symbol of wisdom.

Sometimes client resistance is a figment of our imagination. The problem lies not with what the client is doing to avoid our well-meaning help but with something in us that is interfering with our being more patient, forgiving, and accepting.

Um. Uh. No. One of the basic rules of therapy is that the client talks. When that convention is broken, all else becomes chaos. Occasionally we do work with people, often children, who are not all that verbal, who answer questions in monosyllables if they answer at all, who are uncertain and indecisive, and who can outwait us. We can try any trick in the book—staring contests, interrogations, monologues, card tricks—and we will still end up with virtual silence. With children it is easier because there are still many non-verbal options in the ways time can be spent constructively.

With overly passive or withdrawn adults, a single hour can last years. I think the clock actually slows down—if not downright stops—when these people enter the room.

Something in their hormones must impede time. We feel, at first, like vaudeville entertainers trying to get a laugh. We could sing, dance, probably do a striptease, and the silent client would merely watch indulgently.

> *"So what brings you here?"*
> *"Not sure."*
> *(Kick in active listening.) "You're feeling uncertain and confused."*
> *"Uh huh."*
> *(Wait him out. Silence for four minutes.)*
> *(Active listening again.) "It's difficult for you to talk here."*
> *"Uh huh."*
> *(Try again. Reassurance.) "I, uh, mean with a complete stranger most people find it hard to get started."*
> *"Yes."*
> *(Open-ended questioning.) "Can you tell me a little bit about what is bothering you?"*
> *"My mother."*
> *(Persistence.) "That* is *a little bit. How about some details?"*
> *"She doesn't understand."*

Finally. A breakthrough! The session will drag along at its own interminable pace. Once there is a hint of feeling, an opinion, a concern, we slowly and determinedly explore its shape and form, build and connect previous disclosures.

Eventually we help these people to open up more. But it takes *so* much work.

Equally difficult is the client who talks incessantly but rarely says much and never listens. These clients also have the power to slow down the clock. They have been compulsive talkers for so long that they are virtually impervious to interruptions, confrontations, snoring, gags—everything but fire alarms. Some of these folks eventually find their way into Congress, but the rest end up in therapy because nobody else can stand to listen to them.

Occasionally, when they draw a breath, take a drink, or pause to write a check, they will let the therapist talk for a minute—even a few minutes if she can talk fast—but they will continue with the monologue after this interruption. Amazingly enough, at the start of the next session the client will remember exactly where she left off and will continue as if the week lasted but a moment. Naturally, the client's intent is to prevent hearing anything that might be unpleasant. Eventually, with patience and persistence, we can get the client to change once trust is established.

With the silent or excessively verbal client, the therapist is required to do more, which is to do less. The more we attempt to manage and control the sessions, the longer the obstructive behavior will continue. We can well understand this intellectually but still may be unable or unwilling to restrain our impulse to control. To sit with someone hour after hour after hour and really be with him while he is off in his own world is a Herculean task.

But I Don't Have a Drug Problem. Substance abusers are among those clients who improve only as long as they are in the office. Once they leave, they resort to past habits of getting high to avoid their pain. We face an uphill battle, since therapy can never compete with the instantaneous pleasure that a drug can provide. It is hard enough to counteract the effects of past trauma and the usual defensive reactions. Once the ploys of a skilled alcoholic or drug addict are added to the scene, the therapist who really thinks he can make a difference before the client is ready to change may end up an addict himself. In addition to the abuser's denial that he has a drug or drinking problem, and added on to all of his manipulation, deceit, and sneaking around are the physiological effects. This client is probably physically addicted and psychologically dependent, and he may be experiencing some deterioration and memory loss. The need to escape is much stronger than the need to understand. Avoidance wins over confrontation.

Substance abuse counseling and Alcoholics Anonymous emerged as specialties largely because traditional therapy was not working with the chemically dependent client. As long as she has her Valium, cocaine, or wine to ease the emotional discomfort and pain, she has very little incentive to work on the underlying problems.

Even a relatively harmless drug like marijuana can effectively sabotage any attempts a therapist may make to help a client take constructive action. As long as the client can stay high, locked in his room watching television and munching popcorn, he is not going to be very motivated to do anything that requires much energy.

Clients with drug and alcohol problems who are unwilling to admit their dependency typify the kind of work that can be incredibly frustrating for the therapist. Since the likelihood of success is minimal, the therapist's own feeling of impotence may reflect the client's powerlessness.

Sorry to Bother You at Home. The fastest way to get any therapist's attention is with a panicky 3:00 A.M. phone call. It is hard to say what actually precipitates the late night call because by the time we are fully awake we are already five minutes into the conversation. The gist of it is: (1) Did I wake you up? (2) Sorry to bother you. (3) You said I could call if I needed to. (4) This is kind of an emergency.

Phone calls at home, one of an array of devious ploys common to the borderline client, are irritating but unavoidable. Those who are severely depressed or prone to panic need to have the reassurance that they can call if they absolutely have to. But the therapist should effectively communicate that such an option should be the last resort. Two or three calls per year are probably not a nuisance. Anything more than a few per year may be considered a form of cruel and unusual punishment.

Success with Difficult Cases

Many therapists may be underpaid, overworked, and unappreciated, but there is no doubt that the greatest benefit of our work is the pure unadulterated joy we feel when we can see the results of our efforts, particularly in difficult cases. Yalom (1989), for example, describes the magic he felt as he watched and sometimes participated in a client's struggle to overcome debilitating depression. "I was transfixed by the unfolding drama, as each week offered a new, exciting, and entirely unpredictable episode" (p. 134).

Francine, a seriously disturbed woman, was prone to an assortment of self-destructive, manipulative behaviors that easily qualified her for the dreaded "borderline" diagnosis. She called her therapist at home, threatening suicide at regular intervals. She relied on an assortment of means to sabotage her own progress just to get under the therapist's skin. The clinician stayed with the case for several years. She gnashed her teeth, sought the counsel of her colleagues, attended conferences, and read books, trying anything and everything to find the key that might prove helpful. On two separate occasions she referred the woman to other specialists only to find that, like a boomerang, she sailed back into her office with a completely new set of symptoms. I lost touch with this therapist for a few years. When we resumed contact, I asked how Francine was doing. I expected the therapist to roll her eyes skyward or to begin a litany of complaints that I had heard many times in the past. I was, therefore, quite surprised when she broke out into an angelic smile and her eyes sparkled with pride. There had been no single breakthrough, but gradually, ever so slowly and painfully, Francine had made steady if not dramatic progress. It had taken over four years of patient, excruciatingly

difficult work, but now both she and Francine could see an
amazing difference.

"She still drives me to distraction sometimes. But it has
been worth it! I stayed with her. I hung in there when
nobody else would or could. I don't mean to be grandiose,
but I know I saved her life. And by doing so, I saved a part of
my own."

Dealing with Problem Patients

A significant number of us probably entered the profession
because we like to be needed, to have people depend on us.
It is therefore ridiculous for us to complain when clients
exhibit exactly those qualities of neediness, dependency,
helplessness, and manipulation that they came to us to cure.
We must expect a certain amount of intrusion, of having
people smother us with their demands and even invade our
lives with their late night cries of anguish. We should not be
surprised at the lengths a disturbed person will go to get the
attention he equates with love.

Several principles should be followed in dealing with
any problem client.

1. Determine whether the problem is with the client or
    with us. In many cases it is our own impatience and
    need for control that leads to unnecessary struggles
    and conflict.
2. Respect the purpose and function of resistance and
    client defenses. It is safe to assume that the client's
    irritating or manipulative behavior has served him

well for quite some time. The fact that we are feeling annoyed and off balance is evidence that this behavior is working with us as well.

3. When feeling trapped, follow the principles of the "reflective practitioner" that allow a scientist, an architect, a manager, or a therapist to restructure a problem in such a way that a different set of actions is possible.

4. Do not try to cure the incurable. It is necessary for us to accept our own limits and share with the client the responsibility for the success of treatment.

5. Acknowledge that the client is operating under different rules from what you would prefer. Do not retaliate in anger. Retain your compassion and caring at the same time you enforce appropriate boundaries.

6. Remain as flexible as possible. Patients test our patience precisely because they require treatment that is more innovative than we are used to. Allow so-called "difficult" clients to help stimulate your own creative capacities.

7. When all else fails, allow the clients to keep their dysfunctional behavior. It is *theirs* to keep or lose as they see fit. When they are ready to change, they will do so. Our job is to help them get ready—on *their* schedule.

All of the client patterns presented in this chapter make our lives more difficult but more challenging. The key to preventing boredom and burnout, to surviving in the field with the minimum of negative personal consequences, is to do only what we can—no more and no less.

chapter 6

BOREDOM
AND BURNOUT

Of all the problems a therapist encounters — from someone who wants to jump out a window to someone who is trying to jump out of his skin — none is more difficult than the challenge of staying energized toward one's work. If burnout is caused by an overload of stimulation, then boredom is caused by its absence — at least in terms of subjectively perceived experience. Both involve a discrepancy between what one is giving and what one is receiving. The first part of this chapter will discuss the phenomenon of therapist ennui and tedium; the following section will cover overstimulation, emotional exhaustion, and a broken spirit. In both boredom and burnout the clinician experiences a loss of motivation, energy, control, and direction. These conditions, if left untreated, can become chronic and incurable.

About Boredom

Boredom involves a loss of interest and momentum, either temporarily or chronically. Although it is a state of incredible discomfort, it also serves to rest the mind and spirit to give them time to rejuvenate (Sinclair, 1982).

People have quite literally died of boredom, and perhaps an intolerance for sameness leads others to the fireworks of madness. Boredom is nature's way of saying "Get back to work!" If people felt content with staleness and with doing nothing productive, our species would die out. We have instinctual urges to procreate and preserve our gene pool, to protect and provide for our offspring. And we have urges and ambition to have more, more, more of what we already have—not because we need new things, but because of that voice within us that protests against contentment.

Kierkegaard (1944) believed boredom to be the root of all evil. He was the first to recognize both its motivating and its destructive nature. Boredom creates a void that is frequently filled with reckless thrill seeking, consumerism, and drugs. When a therapist is bored, she is most vulnerable to the hazards of the profession previously enumerated.

When work becomes routine and predictable, when stimulation is minimal, when a person dislikes her own company and that of others, boredom will seep in to motivate some action. It is less a condition than a way of viewing the world.

Boredom can be caused by a collapse of meaning (Healy, 1984). Once upon a time there was a therapist who wished to save the world. He had a diploma, a jacket with patches on the elbows, a leather chair, and the best of intentions. Then he discovered that most of his clients did not want his help and that the rest of the people in the world went to someone else. Day after day he said the same things to his clients and they said the same things to him. He said, "If you're so miserable why don't you change?" They said, "I can't." So time went on. His elbow patches became frayed. And so did his patience.

He began to feel more and more confined by his leather chair; by this time it had lost most of its stuffing. The diploma had yellowed. And his clients stopped saying "I can't" and started saying "I won't." This did not seem to him to be much progress. His prison walls grew closer.

"If it's prison we're in, we righteous helpers, what are we charged with? Breaking and entering with the intention of doing good? Felonious assumption of personal responsibility? Selling water by the river? And what is our defense? Early conditioning? They made me read *Helper Rabbit* every night until I was eight, your Honor. In my house, the cry 'Help!' was an order not a plea" (Ram Dass & Gorman, 1985, p. 125).

Boredom has its benefits, as sensory deprivation experiments will attest. Those athletes who run or swim or bike in ultramarathons for eight hours at a time can also testify to what endless repetition can teach. A long-distance swimmer reports: "You drop into a hypnotic trance. It's not only that you're doing something for eight or ten or twenty hours, but also your communication is cut off. I wear tight rubber caps on my ears; I can't hear very well at all. The goggles just fit over my eyes and I'm turning my head sixty times every minute, so I don't see very much. I don't have time in that eighth of a second that the breath lasts to focus on anything. A lot of childhood and sexual images go through my mind—quick, dreamlike flashes that come like a picture on a movie screen. When I've finished a swim I feel like I know myself better" (Smith, 1976, p. 48).

While we are bored there is time "to strip away our character armor, shed layer after layer of imposed motivations and values, and circle closer to our unique essence" (Keen, 1977, p. 80). It is a time to stand naked and confront one's pain without distractions or diversions. World-class runners are able to simulate a perfect state of boredom in their quest for optimal performance. They refuse to retreat into fantasy when the pain becomes intense but instead stay with the discomfort and pain: "I not only pay attention to my body as I run, but I also constantly remind myself to relax, hang loose, not tie up" (Morgan, 1978, p. 45). Pounding the pavement mile after mile, hour after hour, they concentrate only on the nothingness of where they are—the placement of the foot, the pace of breathing, the swing of arms. They excel because they are willing to put themselves in that place where there is nowhere else to escape to.

Therapist Vulnerability to Boredom

The experience of boredom is, in part, affected by a person's conception of time. Those who are clock-watchers (as therapists tend to be), who are constantly aware of how time progresses, find themselves waiting more often for things to happen. Their involvement in life is regulated by what the clock dictates. The nature of a job that requires the precise timing of a conversation to the minute, with frequent (five to ten times per hour) checks of the clock, makes therapists much more vulnerable to the subjective flow of time. Since boredom is most likely to occur when time seems to slow down, clock-watchers, by inclination and training, are more aware of this phenomenon.

Where people have a radically different conception of time, in Latin American cultures, for example, boredom is experienced with less frequency. Ask a person on the street what time it is, and rather than hearing the precise voice of a person with a digital watch, "8:48," you will hear a gravelly and unconcerned "about 9:00" with an accompanying shrug to indicate "What's the difference?" In Latin cultures there is a great respect for the present and less concern for the future. Nothing is more important than what you are doing now — talking to a dog, finishing a conversation, watching one of the frequent car accidents. Therefore, regardless of what the clock says, whatever you are currently involved in should not be rushed. Time will wait; and if it will not, who cares?

At the most prestigious university in Peru, I taught a seminar for the country's most motivated and talented students. Naturally, I was excited by this opportunity. As is my habit, I arrived a few minutes early to orient myself to the classroom (I had been bored waiting in my office staring at the clock). The class was to start at 9:00 A.M. At precisely that time I found myself standing before a room full of empty chairs. At 9:20 the first student arrived; by 9:35 the room was half full. Confused but irritated, I began my lecture—only to find it interrupted every few minutes by another student casually strolling in. At 10:30 I had planned a break, and with great firmness, in careful and clear Spanish, I urged the students to be back by 10:40. I knew I was in for trouble when I noticed nobody was wearing a watch. By 11:15 we were again assembled, which left me forty-five minutes to cover three hours worth of material. I stopped a student after class to find out how the best and brightest ever learn anything if they are never in class. She looked at me as if I were pitiful creature and patiently explained that it is the way of her country for students to learn in any form that is spontaneously available. She, for example, was late to class because she was involved in a heated argument with another student over some obscure theory. Did I honestly expect her to abruptly end the discussion just to rush to my class? My own experience with boredom came to an end at that moment (at least while I was living in Peru). Thereafter I was taught by my students to appreciate whatever is happening at the moment. To interrupt the flow by consulting a watch is sacrilege.

Csikszentmihalyi (1975) observed exactly this phenomenon while researching the experience of boredom among rock climbers, surgeons, chess players, and dancers. If one of these individuals interrupted his activity to consider time, the intense enjoyment, the immense sensation of flow ceased. Flow occurs only when there is a heightened concentration without effort, when the activity is perfectly balanced between boredom and anxiety, when there is a loss of time and space so that the person becomes that activity. Boredom is impossible for those who are so totally involved in what they are doing that they become that action.

A rock climber: *"You are so involved in what you are doing [that] you aren't thinking of yourself as separate from that activity" [p. 39].*

A chess player: *"When the game is exciting, I don't seem to hear nothing — the world seems to be cut off from me and all there is to think about is the game" [p. 40].*

These descriptions are hardly unfamiliar to us. When we are totally focused in a session, when our words flow forth, when we become the client, when we forget about the room and the chairs, when there is an absence of thought, we experience flow. The session ends too quickly. And we have done our best work even if we cannot recall what we did.

But when we lose the sense of challenge, when we think we know where things are going, boredom infects us. Time seems to stand still. We feel embarrassed by the number of times we have looked at the clock. After planning our dinner menu in our head, calculating our income to date, going off into fantasy land, we notice with a start that someone is talking. "What are you doing here? Why don't you go home?" It is the repetition that is so difficult to tolerate, not only in the similarity of client complaints but in the therapeutic messages we relay. Rational-emotive therapy, for example, can be infuriatingly repetitive in its execution. Even Ellis (1972, p. 119) admits: "I have seen myself at times doing the same thing over and over with clients and have recognized that this is a pain in the ass, this is something I don't greatly like."

Burton (1972) points out that therapists have a particularly difficult time dealing with boredom and so chose a lifestyle that permits a variety of tasks, allows them to get to the heart of problems quickly, and grants them the opportunity to work with very interesting and very strange people. He claims therapists seldom feel bored because they get to hear such titillating secrets from clients who try very hard to be entertaining. The people who march through our offices are indeed unique and individual, yet after years of practice many of the voices sound the same.

A marriage counselor: *"If I hear another husband say he'll do anything to save his marriage but he doesn't have time this week to schedule an appointment . . ."*

A psychiatrist: *"They all want drugs. They come in prepared to do a song and dance showing how sick they are and hoping for relief from some magic pill they think I'm hoarding."*

A psychologist: *"I've done over 4,000 WISC-R's in the last several years. I do them in my sleep. Sure every kid is different, but the damn questions never change."*

A social worker: *"I don't know how many visits I've made to the homes of abused children. It's always the same. I go in and interview the parents, who swear the kid slipped in the bathtub, then admit maybe they did try to teach her a lesson but they'll never do it again. 'You've got to teach these kids they can't walk all over you.' 'Yes, Mr. Walker, but your daughter is eighteen months old. What did she do,* crawl *all over you?' They never get the point and they'll never change. The kid will go to a foster home and probably get beaten by someone else. Maybe a long time ago I found this interesting. Now it's just frustrating and boring."*

English (1972, p. 95) recounts his experiences with boredom in therapy work: "There have been patients I liked to see and treat and some I dreaded to see, some who amused me, some who bored me to distraction. Some could put me to sleep, and I use the word *put* rather than say I went to sleep on them. Because I would find myself thinking, 'How sleepy I am. When the patient leaves I'll take a nap for sure!' But when he departed the office I couldn't go to sleep for the life of me."

One therapist comments that when she feels bored in therapy it usually is because she wants to cut herself off from issues that are threatening. I like that premise because it assumes a degree of control on our part. When a session or a meeting becomes tedious and drags on endlessly, we can look first toward ourselves—what are we hiding from inside this cloak of disinterest?

A second possible explanation for our boredom is that there are people walking around who are objectively, intrinsically, completely devoid of spirit and energy. Some clients come to our offices because they cannot find anyone else who will listen to them. They speak in monotones. They may be alexithymic, incapable of describing internal thoughts and feelings. They are concrete, repetitive, utterly predictable in what they do and how they do it.

These people are thankfully rare. They will test the patience and compassion of any therapist because they do not respond very well to either subtle nudges or nuclear explosions intended to move them toward being more expressive. There is even some question as to whether, neurologically, they have the capacity to be so.

The third possibility when we encounter boredom in our work has less to do with the client, or with the particular issues that are present, than with our own narcissistic demands for stimulation. Although we may be reluctant to admit it, many of us selected this kind of work because we are entertained by the voyeuristic delights of being privy to people's private lives. It is like cable television, each channel a window into a different life. But then one channel gives us identical programming each time we tune in—maybe a fishing show—and we feel cheated: "You are not doing your job! Don't you know you are supposed to go out there in the world and do fun stuff and then come back and tell me about it?"

Boredom, in this third case, results from our own expectations of how clients should perform for us. It is also the situation we can do the most about. People who appear chronically boring believe they are essentially unlovable and have discovered a very effective way to keep others at a distance. Our job, then, is to love them in spite of their attempts to keep us at a distance. This is easier said than done, however, for to do so we must stretch ourselves beyond the limits of our patience and concentration.

Boredom and the Avoidance of Risks

On one end of the continuum is a therapist steeped in boredom—demoralized, dissatisfied, restless, and weary. On the other end is someone who has become timid, irresolute, and fearful of taking risks. Just as change in clients is stymied by a reluctance to act differently or experiment with new modes of being, so, too, do some therapists tend toward safety, security, and predictability at the expense of growth.

Therapists can avoid constructive risking in a number of ways. Here we are not talking about reckless thrill seeking but rather about those occasional opportunities to take an unknown route and end up in a very different place. Reluctance to expose oneself to hazard and danger, unless the perceived gain seems worth the potential loss, is sensible. But much more than the desire to protect ourselves from needless jeopardy is a pathological avoidance of risk that may reveal us to be impotent, ineffective, or inadequate. When one is secure and comfortable, it takes some real incentive to convince her to venture out into the cold. We may therefore be just as guilty as everyone else of postponing action until it becomes absolutely necessary and of avoiding the unknown when it is at all possible.

Therapists who play it safe in their work may remain basically satisfied with their moderate gains. They will do just enough to get the job done, but not enough to ever produce dramatic results. Under the guise of protecting their client's welfare, they will avoid confrontation and conflict, preferring instead to move at a pace consistent with the client's own tolerance for boredom. They will wait and wait, knowing that waiting has its therapeutic value and that most clients will get better on their own or in spite of what we do. Such therapists will say only what they have said before. They will do only what has been tried before. Any departure from the formula must be preceded by a consultation of the works of their favorite authority.

Certainly it is neither appropriate nor helpful to advocate risky therapeutic interventions to appease some restless spirit in the therapist. On the contrary, those who are able to satisfy their needs for stimulation and excitement in their personal lives have no interest in using their clients as guinea pigs in experimentation for its own sake. Therapists, in fact, have an obligation to protect people at risk from exposure to unnecessary dangers. But there are many ways a clinician may safely and responsibly try new intervention strategies without jeopardizing the client's safety.

Solutions to Boredom

Although boredom is an inevitable if uninvited guest, it need not stay long. Yet when the clinician feels apathetic and helpless it may become a permanent resident. Sometimes, despite a fervent desire for renewal, boredom nevertheless hangs on.

In Csikszentmihalyi's (1990) research on flow as an antidote to boredom, he concludes that finding greater purpose in our work is the key. "The psychic entropy peculiar to the human condition involves seeing more to do than one can actually accomplish and feeling able to accomplish more than what conditions allow" (p. 228). Excitement and stimulation result from the *perception* of challenge matched to our abilities. This is one of the main messages we teach to our clients — any emotional state, boredom most of all, is the logical consequence of our chosen cognitive activity.

The primary cure for boredom in therapy is to focus on the uniqueness of each case, the individuality of each client, and the opportunity for growth in every encounter. When our minds function routinely and interventions have become mechanical, we experience tedium. When I catch myself feeling blasé about the real magic that is transpiring in my involvement with a client, I make a deliberate shift in my perception. If I first shift my position in the chair and concentrate on my breathing and on my posture, if I go back to the basics I learned as a student, I find that something wonderful takes place. The client becomes more special, her words carry more power, the whole experience becomes energized. I can feel the new energy, and so can the client. As she notices my renewed interest, she begins to feel and act more interestingly, not to entertain me and release me from my boredom, but because I value our time together more. She begins to believe that she is more exciting. The changes are, at first, very subtle: I forget to watch the clock and the session runs over.

Another practitioner relates his strategy for avoiding staleness in his work: "I have never been bored. . . . I consider myself very fortunate to be doing such interesting work, particularly when I can experience a degree of falling in love with a patient. This is not a threat to my marital commitment but rather is a further installment on the resolving of my romance with my parents and my siblings. When I can no longer fall in love with patients to some degree, I will be approaching the end of my vitality as a therapist" (Warkentin, 1972, pp. 258–259).

Other therapists successfully immunize themselves against boredom by taking on challenging cases that do not permit a lax attitude. It also helps to be under the supervision of someone who helps keep us off balance, humble, and comfortably confused. Boredom thus can be kept at bay by working consciously and deliberately to keep things fresh, and especially by looking for meaning in the things we do.

About Burnout

Burnout is the single most common personal consequence of practicing therapy. No matter how skilled a practitioner is at avoiding other occupational hazards (including boredom), there will be some period of time—a day, a week, a month, or all eternity—in which serious consideration will be given to leaving the field. Perhaps it will be one of those days when successive "no-shows" combine with an irate phone call from an irrational parent. Or maybe one of those weeks in which you discover that the supervisor you liked has moved on and the colleague you do not like has just been promoted over you to that position. Or one of those months in which your tires are slashed by an ex-client you thought you had helped and your ego is repeatedly slashed by peers trying to undermine your authority, referral sources who have lost confidence, a supervisor who feels threatened by your superior intellect, and clients who will no longer return your phone calls.

The question, then, is not who will experience burnout but how long the next episode will last. It is the nature of the human condition in general, and the therapist condition in particular, to experience ebbs and flows in life satisfaction. Ours is a very emotional business with many highs and lows. Sometimes we feel as close to being a god as any mortal can—powerful, elegant, graceful, wise—and other times we feel so totally inept we wonder how we can be allowed to continue to practice. No matter how many people we have helped, deep inside there is a sickening feeling that we will never be able to do it again. For the life of me I do not really know what I did the last time. And when a new client comes in, sits down, presents his case, and then waits expectantly for my assessment, there is always a minute of panic in which I stall and think to myself: "I don't have any idea what's going on, nor do I have the foggiest notion of what is going to help this gentleman." Then I take a deep breath, jump in, and say something, anything, if only "I don't know yet what is happening, but I'm sure we'll figure it out together."

Symptoms of Burnout

During periods of stress and burnout, therapists are in greater jeopardy of breaching ethical conduct and thus are advised to monitor themselves carefully. We risk greater vulnerability to sexual improprieties: feeling sexually aroused by a client, discussing sexual issues based on our own interest rather than on client needs, meeting clients outside the office for supposedly legitimate reasons, or asking clients to engage in certain sexual behaviors so that we may enjoy them vicariously (Pope & Bouhoutsos, 1986). Sixty-three percent of practicing therapists admit they know of a colleague who is seriously burned out. Thirty-two percent acknowledge that they have personally experienced this condition (Wood et al., 1985).

Burnout, at first glance, looks like plain old depression—loss of energy and motivation, feelings of helplessness and futility—and it most certainly *is* depressing. "It is the rising tide of disillusionment, hopelessness and exhaustion that gradually swamps all the good intentions, enthusiasm and sense of meaning that once-dedicated people brought to their work" (Wylie & Markowitz, 1992, p. 20). Yet whereas depression is an all-pervasive state, burnout is centered around and sparked by our work.

A number of fairly specific behavioral indices of acute burnout have been described by several authors. The following discussion of the symptoms of, causes of, and cures for burnout was inspired by input from Freudenberger (1975); Bach (1979); Edelwich and Brodsky (1980); Pines, Aronson, and Kafry (1981); Maslach (1982, 1986); and Guy (1987). Because burnout is often a disorder of rapid and dramatic onset, it is easy to recognize. The symptoms that follow are the clearest indications of an incipient problem.

- There is a general unwillingness to discuss work in social and family circles. When queried by friends about what is new at the office, the therapist's eyebrows rise, shoulders shrug, but nothing comes out. In fact, the therapist, if she makes any response at all, may snort and then use all her therapeutic skills to deftly change the focus to someone or something else.
- There is a reluctance to call the office or answering service for messages and a resistance to returning calls. It is as if there could not possibly be any message waiting that is worth getting excited about. In his most pessimistic state, the burned-out therapist may think that a message can bring only one of three possibilities: (1) someone is canceling an appointment at the last

minute, leaving a gaping hole in the therapist's schedule during the middle of the day, (2) a new referral has called and wants to be squeezed into an already overloaded week, or (3) a life insurance agent has called to talk to the therapist about his inevitable death.

- When a client does call to cancel, the therapist celebrates with a bit too much enthusiasm. Dancing and singing in the hallway is a dangerous sign of advanced deterioration. Whispers under one's breath such as "Thank God!" and other expressions of relief are certainly more socially appropriate, but they are equally indicative of professional dread.

- One of the best clues to burnout in a therapist is when several clients complain of similar symptoms. When there is a rash of complaints about hopelessness, frustration, pessimism, and doubt in the therapeutic process, the clinician may silently be in agreement. Since clients resonate our faith and beliefs, they also sense and imitate our despair. A frustrated and unmotivated therapist does little to promote growth in his clients. It is hard to imagine that his clients are going to do more than go through the motions of their treatment. If they improve, it will be largely in spite of their therapist rather than because of his help. In fact, some clients will get better just to escape the punitive drudgery of their sessions.

- Daydreaming and escapist fantasy are common. During sessions, the therapist's eyes are inadvertently drawn to the window or door. It takes constant vigilance to stay with the client. Yet, in spite of these good intentions, the mind drifts away to some other place and time. During idle periods, the escapist thinking continues as the therapist imagines herself rescuing princes in distress or lying on a beach in Eleuthera.

- The alarm clock is less a signal to begin the day than an order to resume one's sentence. There is reluctance to get out of bed, and excuses to avoid getting started abound. During the day the therapist functions at half-speed and is lethargic, apathetic, disconnected. Much time is devoted to coffee breaks and ploys to stall action.

- As in all instances of prolonged stress, therapists are prone to anesthetizing themselves with self-prescribed medications. In some cases legal drugs like Xanex and Valium are used with regularity. More frequently, stressed therapists resort to abusing the substance of their choice: marijuana, alcohol, or, for those who are more affluent, cocaine.

- Cynicism is manifested in a number of ways. To colleagues and friends, the therapist may make a number of deprecating remarks about clients, ridiculing them for their weaknesses, joking about their helplessness. And the therapist may find a commentary running through her head during sessions: "If you only knew what a fool you look like," "That's what you think," "You are so boring no wonder your wife left you," "I don't care what you do, what are you asking me for?"

- Sessions lose their spark, their excitement, their zest and spontaneity. There is very little laughter, little movement. The room feels stagnant. Voices become monotones. There are lots of yawns and uncomfortable silences. Sessions end early.

- The therapist falls behind in paperwork and billings. Progress notes, fee sheets, treatment plans, and quarterly summaries pile up. During the best of times such chores are handled with less than joy; the burned-out therapist may spend more time complaining about the forms to be completed than actually completing them. Management intervenes to slap the therapist's hand, often with other punitive measures to enforce compliance to organizational rules. The therapist eventually capitulates—but with a cursory effort designed to merely play the game.

- During leisure time there is a distinct preference for passive entertainment. Watching television is easier than getting out in the world to do something. "I'm so tired of having to be responsible for other people's lives that I want someone else to take charge of mine." "I don't feel like doing much tonight."

- The therapist is so emotionally tied to his work that an active social life is completely precluded. He has difficulty relinquishing control, feeling he must do everything himself. He experiences excessive internal pressure to succeed and an overidentification with his clients to the point of losing his own identity.

■ Last, but hardly least, the therapist is reluctant to explore the causes and cures of his burned-out condition. Rather than making needed changes or confronting the emotional difficulties that are blocking satisfaction, he prefers to make excuses and criticize others for the problem. Much of what a therapist does involves interrupting this destructive cycle in others; thus, the final symptom of burnout is an inability or unwillingness to apply one's therapeutic wisdom to oneself. There is probably some ironic justice in creating so devastating a punishment for those who practice therapy in a spirit of hypocrisy and self-neglect.

Causes of Burnout

Depending on one's immunological system, recuperative powers, and work environment, therapist stagnation can be either a temporary nuisance or a tragic flaw that requires a career change. Several influences determine the extent and duration of this occupational and personal crisis.

Predisposing Factors. It is the nature of the human life cycle to experience periods of relative calm alternating with spurts of disorientation and subsequent growth. Freud, Erikson, Piaget, Havighurst, Kohlberg, Levinson, and Loevinger have documented how development proceeds according to an orderly sequence of stages that build on prior adaptive experiences. In the career of a therapist, as well, there are predetermined stages of growth that are facilitated by such variables as formal training, critical incidents, and exposure to theories, mentors, and experiences. According to a developmental conception of occupational growth, certain predictable "hot spots" will emerge. Therapists are most vulnerable during life-cycle transitions, during periods of accelerated metabolic changes, and after decade-long intervals in between theoretical changes. Professionals who work in isolation or who tend to be loners are at greater risk, as are those who are overly idealistic, who have overly high expectations for what they can do, or who do this kind of work because of a longing for greater intimacy in their lives (Farber, 1983a; Guy, 1987).

Some therapists are at risk not only because of developmental evolution but because of certain personality characteristics. Those with a low tolerance for frustration and for ambiguity, a high need for approval and for mandatory control, and rigid patterns of thought are going to be in for greater turbulence. One social worker, for example, has been practicing orthodox psychoanalysis for twenty years. He subscribes to all the appropriate journals, attends conventions religiously, and is proud of the fact he has not changed his style since he completed his own analysis decades previously. He resists change even within his sheltered professional circles and scoffs at ego psychology or Jungian analysis as too revisionist. He actually does very little in his sessions, although he can talk to a colleague for hours about all the fascinating things that are happening. He is often frustrated because he sees little progress in his clients and receives so little feedback from them concerning how they feel toward him.

The seeds of self-destruction may first be sown, if not fertilized as well, in graduate school. Therapists get themselves in trouble with unrealistic expectations and unreasonable goals. No matter what the textbooks and professors say, you are not going to cure schizophrenia by reflecting feelings, and you are not going to wipe out chronic depression by disputing a few irrational beliefs. Naive beginners enter the field prepared to conduct neat, elegant, organized therapy in ten sessions or less with people who will change fast, pay lots of money, and be exceedingly grateful. It takes several years for them to realize that some clients will always be the same no matter what you do; you will never get rich or famous being a therapist; and most of the time you will be unappreciated and overworked.

Bureaucratic Constraints. There are factors within most organizational structures that may make for efficient operations, happy boards of directors, and balanced budgets but are hardly conducive to staff morale. Paperwork is just one example of a product that pleases funding and accreditation agencies but drives clinical personnel up the wall. For every session of therapy that is conducted, the therapist may spend fifteen minutes describing in sickening detail what the client talked about, what interventions were used, how that particular session contributed to the overall treatment goals, and how the client felt after he left. In some settings all this material must be repeated again and again for summaries, insurance forms, case reports, and departmental files.

Some mental health agencies, hospitals, social service departments, universities, and clinics are notorious for their political wars. Power struggles are waged not only among department heads and within the administrative hierarchy, but especially among the different professional groups. Psychiatrists, social workers, family therapists, counselors, psychologists, psychiatric nurses, and mental health technicians often stick together in their respective groups, each with their own biases toward others. The result of this often intense competition is an environment in which people vie for control, status, recognition, and power. In such a setting it is not surprising that people choose to drop out.

Prejudices, biases, and discrimination only add to the frustration of a clinician functioning in a bureaucracy. Promotions and raises are based less often on merit than on credentials, skin color, and sex. Some therapists give up because they feel their careers are at a dead end. They may be able to continue improving themselves as clinicians and administrators, but there is little they can do to alter their background, their race, their religion, or their sex.

Even the most dedicated and well-meaning practitioner who has successfully avoided all the previously mentioned traps may find it difficult to resist the contagious effects of others' disillusionment. When the institutional norm is to complain about the food, it is difficult to enjoy a meal. When other staff members complain about how they have been abused by the administration, it is hard to go about one's business as if others care for your welfare. In the worst of circumstances it takes a new recruit but a few weeks to lose her initial surge of enthusiasm.

Emotional Stress. Most of the problems contributing to burnout are centered less around the actual daily work than around the therapist's unresolved emotional difficulties (Dai, 1979). Some professionals invest their egos too intensely in the outcome of their work, an outcome that depends very much on the client's motivation and behavior. Therefore, they may attempt to do too much in the sessions, taking too much responsibility for filling silences, providing immediate relief of symptoms, and generating insight. The more control the therapist takes, the less the client assumes. The more the therapist does, the less there is for the client to do.

This is not to say the therapist is justified in assuming a passive, detached, observatory role that allows the client to flounder aimlessly. Certainly we share some responsibility with the client for planning the content of sessions, providing some input into choices, and gently helping to generate a degree of self-understanding and subsequent action. The problem arises when, out of a personal sense of importance, the therapist feels a genuine, gut-level stake in what the client does and how fast she does it.

Emotional factors enter the picture not only for the therapist who tries too hard but for the one who overidentifies with a client's situation. No matter how many times I hear a young client cry out in anger and frustration at being teased by his peers, I feel the pain every time. As the little guy goes on to relate the incident of striking out for the third time in front of his heckling teammates, I can feel myself actually shaking. I was one of those kids sent into exile in right field.

Often the sutures closing up an old wound fail to hold against the onslaught of emotional issues presented by clients. Sometimes the best we can hope for is constant vigilance: "This client is not me. This client is *not* me. I am sitting over *here* in the more comfortable chair. I am being paid to sit here, to listen, to react, but *not* to get into my own stuff."

A final emotional issue worth mentioning concerns those therapists who lack family support for their work. Helping professionals require much nurturance, understanding, and demonstrations of affection. After giving and giving all day long, a therapist can come home with a short fuse and a long list of demands. Tender loving care is indicated until he or she returns to the land of the living. This is especially true for women in the field, who often must contend with more than their fair share of family and household chores in addition to a full work schedule. Single parents also shoulder a disproportionate burden of financial hardships, car pooling, laundry, and late nights cleaning house.

Cures for Burnout

Just as with our clients, denial is the major impediment to successful treatment of burnout. From his work with overstressed mental health professionals, physicians, dentists, nurses, clergy, pharmacists, and police officers, Freudenberger (1986) noted marked reluctance on the part of these professionals to acknowledge that their lives were out of control. In the face of dwindling caseloads, client or colleague complaints, family concerns or obviously dysfunctional behavior (substance abuse, depression, sexual problems, financial irresponsibility, psychosomatic complaints) the clinician refuses to admit there is a problem, hoping things will improve on their own. As we know only too well, they rarely do.

Belson (1992) offers some tried and true advice for achieving a raging case of burnout: (1) work long hours, especially at night; (2) see many cases consecutively without breaks; (3) don't take vacations, and when you do, read professional literature and think about your cases; (4) keep doing the same thing the same way; (5) don't have a personal life outside of work, believing that your clients need you too much; (6) believe that you can help everyone all of the time and that when you don't it is your fault.

The result of many of these factors that contribute to burnout is increased isolation and withdrawal on the part of the therapist. Since it often is difficult for professional helpers to ask for help, the self-destructive patterns become more entrenched and more resistant to treatment. Nevertheless, several self-administered preventions and cures can be useful.

Do Therapy Differently. The simplest and most direct way to breathe life into unsatisfying work is either to do something else or to do what you are already doing a little (or a

lot) differently. The booming business of presenting work-
shops and seminars attests to the popularity of this particular strategy, even if the effects are short-lived. After an initial
surge of enthusiasm upon returning from a workshop or
convention, many therapists slip back into the doldrums. A
good speaker can be infectious in her spirit, but just as in
therapy, unless the participant continues to apply the ideas
on a daily basis, regression is likely.

After many years of struggling to sort through the vast
array of theoretical orientations, therapeutic technology,
and conflicting claims, one may feel more secure sticking
with a proven and familiar recipe. Even if we have no
particular objection to learning new concepts, new rules, a
new vocabulary, and a new set of skills, trying something
new seems to mean condemning the old ways to obsoles-
cence. This is hardly the case, since we always retain those
ideas that are still helpful. Nevertheless, until a therapist
encounters discomfort of sufficient magnitude, he will exhibit considerable resistance to radical change. The key,
therefore, is to give oneself permission to change a little at a
time, to experiment, and to be more creative.

One psychologist had been giving his clients relaxation
exercises with great success for years. He had found a proven
formula for creating effective and efficient induction procedures, vivid images, and positive results. His clients were
still improving (though less so in recent months), but he was
feeling much worse. With all the complaints he made about
how stale and boring his work felt, with all the options he
considered in giving up behavioral strategies, it never oc-

curred to him to simply change his exercise instructions. He did not really need to read them any more, but he did so because he did not trust himself to work spontaneously. An unusual example of rigidity, this case highlights the point that a psychoanalyst need not become a Rolfing specialist, nor does a gestalt therapist need to adopt behavior modification in order to re-energize her work.

Doing therapy differently means forcing oneself to venture off into uncharted territory where the destination is less well defined. It means joining the client as a partner in the spiritual odyssey. Most of all it means conquering burnout paradoxically by initially working even harder until it no longer is work at all.

Teach Others. There is a very good reason why so many professors do counseling as an avocation and why so many therapists teach, and it has less to do with generating pocket money than with rejuvenating one's enthusiasm. Therapists teach not only as a way of spreading the gospel and increasing referrals and their reputation, but as a way of giving greater meaning to their clinical work. When you explain to others what you do, how you do it, and why you do it a particular way, you are forced to think through the rationale for every intervention.

An ex-therapist, ex-professor, and now university administrator still works with a few clients just to keep her skills honed and her perspective fresh. She still fights for the opportunity to teach one clinical course each semester even though it means extra work. She does not receive extra compensation, nor do her superiors approve, since it means time away from her office. She does it for her own mental health: "Teaching helps me to be more honest and self-critical. When I talk about what it means to be a good therapist, it helps me to be more that way myself."

Another therapist teaches a graduate-level course even though it means a night away from home each week and only a token honorarium: "I usually get stuck with the classes none of the full-time staff want to teach. But I don't mind. It's a way to get to talk to people in the field who are still eager and fresh. It's a privilege and an honor to work with the really good students. I'd do it for free. I teach this one techniques class that nobody ever likes—not the professors or the students—because it involves making and analyzing verbatim transcripts. My therapy has changed so much since I started studying the work of beginners who know next to nothing. They use low-level and awkward active listening, and yet they are still effective. Since I started going back to the basics in my own work, I'm surprised to find I enjoy it all over again."

A full-time professor relates the impact of teaching on his clinical work: "Questions drive me nuts! The questions some students ask...Like one wise-ass asked me how do I know any of my clients ever really get better. Maybe they're just pretending. Now this guy had no intention of being profound; he was just being silly. I put him off with some appropriate remark. But then I started thinking, really thinking, about the reasons I know for sure that clients really change, not just fake it. The more I thought about it, the better I felt about doing therapy."

Clinicians who do research, give public lectures, publish articles, and write books report similar peak experiences. To teach is to magnify our influence. To teach is to continually evaluate what we do from the perspective of an innocent. We feel greater meaning not only in the single life we help to improve but in how that life helps us to understand and improve the process of change.

Take Personal Responsibility. In every institution in every city of the world, there are therapists who are relatively immune to burnout. They get a tremendous kick out of making a crying child smile or an adult with a plastic smile cry. They stand aloof from the backstabbing, yet they retain their power through their expertise, dependability, and tremendous competence. They take care of themselves and of the people around them. They expect honesty and respect from others. Even in a closed environment we can choose such colleagues as friends.

Corey (1991) suggests that every practitioner take personal responsibility for preventing burnout and maintaining a high level of vitality. Seeking out enthusiastic colleagues is only one of several practical strategies that might include any or all of the following:

- Assume as much responsibility for your own growth as you try to with your clients.

- Use multiple measures of success in your work, not just the client's explicit gratitude. Set limits with demanding clients and colleagues concerning what you are willing to do and what you are not able to do.
- Develop outside interests as a form of renewal—especially activities that exercise parts of your body and mind that go unused during work.

Create Work Breaks. Some therapists are great advocates of work breaks used as buffers against stress, as emotional breathers providing time and space to unwind, and as safety valves to blow off steam (Maslach, 1986). For some practitioners this simply means not scheduling so many appointments consecutively. Other clinicians are more systematic in their efforts. As one person relates, "Since I normally start to drag in the early afternoon and begin asking myself why I am still doing this kind of work after all these years, I have learned to program the hours from 2:00 to 4:00 for my own mental health. I read somewhere that this is the time when most mammals take naps and when most industrial accidents take place. I can believe it. Anyway, I take time out from my day to go for a walk, to work out, or to read a novel."

As a representative of therapists working in schools and agencies, who have less flexibility than in private practice regarding how they structure their time, one professional explains how he keeps burnout at bay: "I build rest periods into my day whenever I can. I might steal a few minutes here and there to meditate or read a magazine. Sometimes when

I have an unexpected cancellation—at this place that happens every day—I force myself to *not* use the time productively. I like to just close the door of my office and play computer games."

Confront the Source of Stress. In many cases job stress results from a specific, identifiable source. The physical environment may be a factor—for instance, sharing space with a coworker. The relationship one has with one's immediate supervisor is another definite possibility. Nothing is more frustrating than an incompetent boss who enjoys having others under his thumb; demands stringent accountability; likes paperwork; sends conflicting orders; invites honest feedback, but only if it is pleasant; and understands very little about therapy. In his first job out of graduate school, a man reports that while he counseled young adolescents in a cubicle without a door or ceiling, his supervisor would listen with her ear to the wall. Every time he said anything to the child she did not agree with, the supervisor would bang on the wall and yell out "Don't tell him that!" When the startled child and fledgling counselor then continued their conversation in a hushed whisper, another bang would ensue followed by the words: "If you two have to be so secretive you shouldn't be talking about whatever you are talking about." The counselor now works as a salesman.

It is always difficult to confront the source of discomfort; sometimes it seems impossible. Excuses for avoiding a confrontation include "It's not so bad," "It's probably the same everywhere," and "Everyone else can handle it." But without taking some risks, nothing will ever change — with clients or with ourselves.

In their study of physician burnout, Coombs and Fawzy (1986) concluded that balance is the key to healthful professional functioning. They refer not only to the age-old problem in medicine of including an appropriate amount of emotional detachment and sensitivity in the work but also to maintaining a balance of the head (intellect), hands (clinical skills), and heart (affective sensitivity). They suggest that when practitioners rely too heavily on one or two of these areas to the exclusion of the third, professional impairment is more likely.

The Impaired Therapist

The process of therapist burnout resembles rust out. Through repeated use, without continual maintenance, any machine will begin to wear out and eventually will cease to function effectively. This same process happens to therapists when they neglect themselves and fail to stay in peak intellectual, emotional, and physical shape.

Approximately 10 percent of practicing therapists are clinically depressed. Another 10 percent have problems with substance abuse. A significant number of clinicians struggle with chronic illness (10 percent) and loneliness (8 percent) (Thoreson, Miller, & Krauskopf, 1989). In several surveys of practicing therapists, between two-thirds and three-quarters of them reported suffering moderate to incapacitating symptoms of depression or anxiety at some time during their careers (Looney, Harding, Blotcky, & Barnhart, 1980; Bermak, 1977; Deutsch, 1985; Thoreson, Budd, & Krauskopf, 1986).

Then there are those who suffer from the usual pedestrian varieties of personality disorder, anxiety, and obsessive-compulsive disorders that led them to seek a profession in which they could "hide." We all know someone in the profession who is seriously disturbed and consequently preys on clients through sexual exploitation, inappropriate value indoctrination, or other forms of pathological manipulation and control.

Dr. Narcissus is one such individual. Like more than a few charming manipulators, he has found the practice of therapy to be a haven in which to seduce people to do his bidding. Once upon a time, he entertained fantasies of being a true savior of humankind. Since he was brighter and better looking than most, and endowed with special talents, he felt he was entitled to accolades from clients and colleagues alike.

In the early days, his clients did not show him sufficient respect, nor did they feel sufficiently grateful for his efforts to help them. Some were even angry and put off by his arrogance. He began to find therapeutic work tedious and unsatisfying. With no other options available to him (like any seriously distressed person, he suffered perceptual distortions that clouded his judgment), he began to experiment with ways to make his work more satisfying.

It started innocently enough with requests that his clients show a little more appreciation. Things eventually escalated to the point where he seduced them emotionally, and a few times sexually. Reasoning in the best tradition of Raskolnikov from *Crime and Punishment* that extraordinary individuals are exempt from the normal laws of mortals, he felt he was doing nothing wrong since he was providing a service to his clients.

After a close call in which a client threatened to file a complaint, and observing an increasingly litigious atmosphere regarding sexual exploitation, he limited himself thereafter to emotional seductions. He manipulated and cajoled as many of his clients as he could to become totally dependent on him. It reached the point where when he went on vacation, several of his clients booked rooms in the same resort at the same time so he could continue to see them.

We are all familiar with colleagues who continue to operate even though they are doing great harm. If we were to confront them directly with suspicions about what we have heard they would seem shocked and indignant. Being distressed, however, does not necessarily mean a professional is impaired (Nathan, 1986). Presumably, it is possible to experience some degree of crisis or trauma in one's life and still conduct one's work, if not superlatively, then at least adequately.

It is unfortunate that when burnout does lead to significant impairment, it is the nature of the therapist's dysfunction to deny that there is anything wrong. There is a hole in the professional's conscience, evidence of sociopathy, or, more often, a kind of blinding attempt to save oneself at the expense of others. It is when one can no longer deal with stress or keep symptoms of burnout under control that a therapist is most likely to engage in unethical conduct or make self-serving decisions that harm others (Stadler, 1990).

Whereas it is unlikely that anyone reading these words is seriously impaired (I suspect such an individual would not be open to confronting the personal nuances of his or her work), there are many among us who can feel themselves slipping, inexorably, toward continued rust out and eventual distress.

The psychologically impaired therapist has probably ignored his problems for months if not years. His energy has been depleted and a sense of cynical hopelessness has set in. He will infect many colleagues as well as his clients before the disease runs its course to retirement, death, or disablement.

To make it easier for therapists to ask for help, a number of state professional societies have organized hot lines for impaired therapists. In an effort to reduce the proliferation of therapists who act out in their sessions as well as to control excessive drug and alcohol abuse among their colleagues, professional therapists stand ready to provide assistance where and when it is needed. We all have a duty and responsibility to promote not only the well-being of our clients and our own mental health but the functioning of our colleagues as well. That boredom and burnout often lead to more severe personal consequences such as depression, drug addiction, suicide, divorce, and the breakdown of professional effectiveness is inevitable. We all entered the helping profession to make a difference in the world. The place to start is with ourselves and then with our peers.

chapter 7

LIES WE TELL OURSELVES

$\int$ome of the negative personal consequences of being a therapist derive less from the pressure of clients, supervisors, and work schedules than they do from some form of self-deceit. Buried deep beneath the polished surface of a professional truthbuster may be an intricate web of lies. Most of them are harmless little fictionalizations we are aware of and choose to ignore. Others are buried deeper, beyond our consciousness, embedded within our system of denial, rationalizations, and distortions.

There are itty-bitty white lies and big black ones. There are lies that are so obviously untruthful that we do not really consider them designed to dupe anyone. There are lies all around us — in the charters and policies and procedures manuals of our facilities; in the minutes of the board meetings and public advisory meetings; in the stated purposes of an organization: not only to help people or make the world a better place, but also to make money, to provide tax write-offs, to pay off political favors, to keep a few people's egos or bellies well fed, or to satisfy some bureaucratic imperative.

We live especially with the lies that our clients bring to us every day. The really honest clients do not even pretend to disguise their fabrications. And we humor them as well, lying when we pretend to believe that they had a happy childhood, that therapy is such fun, or that the check they owe us is in the mail.

We live with such incredible dishonesty in client disclosures and reports—some of them unconscious omissions, others deliberate falsifications—that we sometimes forget the rough fit between a childhood memory and its repetition years later after being squeezed through the mind's protective sieve. This distinction between narrative and historical truth totally debunks the myth of the client as unbiased reporter and therapist as unbiased listener. To support this idea, Spense (1982) reviews the process of therapy in which the client relates an unfinished story in finished form, creating meaning, transitions, and completion of memories that are actually quite muddled. More of the historical truth is lost during the process of translating images into words. Finally, the therapist distorts the truth of what actually occurred even more by supplying contextual assumptions to fill in gaps. Since it is difficult if not impossible to ever find out what really happened in a client's life, given the lapses of memory, language, and perceptual accuracy, we become comfortable with a certain level of deception and half-truth. We settle for an approximation of truth, in our clients and in ourselves. The result of this reality, coupled with a mind trained to detect the intricacies of rationalization and intellectualization, is a therapist who lives under the specter of Truth and Justice. But scratch us and we bleed. We are not all that we appear to be.

Games Therapists Play

We deliberately cultivate our aura of mystery and omnipotence, not to deceive, but to increase our influencing power. No self-respecting wizard or magician, or any professional for that matter, could expect to be effective if he gave away the tricks of his trade. And we have a set of special skills we use to convince the Dorothys in the Land of Oz that we are indeed powerful wizards.

For example, clients are constantly amazed at how we seem to know exactly when the hour is over, as if we had a special internal mechanism to sense the subtle changes of time. After years of practice we are rarely caught unobtrusively glancing at the clock when the client is temporarily distracted.

We disguise our imperfections and lapses as well, believing quite rightly that they would interfere with our image as powerful healers. For example, we have developed an impressive array of options to disguise yawns. As we do not wish the client to know we may feel bored or fatigued, we place the hand in front of the mouth in a pensive pose. Strategically sipping coffee also works quite well.

To counteract the temptation to yawn, another subtle

therapist skill is the ability to look attentive during lapses into personal fantasy. We can keep head nods, furrowed brows, and "uh huhs" going at the same moment we are fighting our own dragons. Of course, sometimes we get caught and the client may explicitly test our powers of concentration with: "Do you know what I mean?" That is the true test of the experienced clinician, which brings us to a whole new category of maneuver: what to do when you did not hear what the client just said. Even the most directive therapist will lapse back into her best Rogerian response: "My opinion is really important to you."

A knowing, mystical follow-up posture will often help to stall for time until we can come up with a more acceptable response. To err may be human, but it is not all that noble for therapists whose power may be undermined by mistakes. A series of defensive ploys is often required for slips when, for example, our interpretations miss the mark. We can always backpedal and redefine the misjudgment as "only a working hypothesis" or "a possible theory," but certainly the client will lose confidence. One clever option is to reluctantly explain that the interpretation was actually a paradoxical maneuver specifically designed to elicit the reaction it did.

Two variations on this theme offer similar responses. Either when the client does not understand something we just said or when we do not understand what the client said, we can act as though it is the client's fault. A stony, quizzical face is quite effective in driving home the point that in close calls the therapist gets the benefit of the doubt. This implicit rule of thumb also allows us to sit silently when we do not know what to do next. The client may feel the responsibility to keep the ball rolling and say something emotional or intelligent.

Perhaps these games are necessary to increase the stature, omnipotence, and influencing capabilities of the therapist—but it is always at the expense of the genuineness, humanness, and presence that are so crucial in being with a client. People respond to us not only because of our professional competence but also because of our uniquely personal aura. The way we smile, laugh, love, and give, the way our eyes twinkle, teach clients as much about themselves as the most sophisticated interventions.

Counterfeit Intelligence

Another self-deception is the most universal of therapist frauds. There we sit amongst our diplomas and memorabilia acting as if we know exactly what we are doing. The collection of books and the wafting air of professionalism attest to our expertise. The client comes in self-possessed and off balance, so what does he know? It takes the average client three to six sessions just to get his bearings, much less to decide whether this professional who comes so highly recommended is really a lightweight.

I can quote chapter and verse in Freud or any of the masters I have studied. I know exactly how to act like a therapist—that is, I have my penetrating stares, monosyllabic grunts, charming smile, and wise demeanor down pat. I know how to ask intelligent questions, to keep the conversation flowing, and, every once in a while, to say something fairly intelligent. If pressed, I can even tell a persistent client what I think his problem is and what he needs to do to make things better. Most of the time, if he follows my direction, he will get much better. But the truth of the matter is that throughout much of the encounter I am actually quite confused, uncertain, indecisive, and awkward. On the stage or in the therapist's chamber, the audience rarely discovers such lapses in performance.

A very prominent and successful psychoanalyst with twenty years of experience admits: "I tell myself that because I've had so many years of experience I can handle whatever walks in the door. But I don't know if I will or I won't. I lie to myself and to my patients to feel the confidence I need to manage a professional practice. In truth I am extremely anxious every time I see a new patient. Will I understand him? Will I make an asshole of myself? Will I make a serious error in judgment? Will I know what to do? No. No. No. But I say to myself and to the client: 'Of course I can help you,' even when I think I can't."

Telling clients that we can help them is assuredly helpful even if it is not strictly true. Favorable expectations and placebo responses are set up principally by the therapist's belief in herself and the process. By communicating confidence, however false it might feel, we establish hope and motivation in the client. We would lose clients very quickly if after every bungled interpretation or misjudgment we muttered under our breath, but within earshot: "Oops. I blew that one." We would never get clients to come back if we were completely honest with them in the first sessions.

In other words, the client may need to believe in this lie and the others to be reviewed in order to get better. No physician in his right mind would ever let his uncertainties slip out, not just because he needs to protect himself from malpractice suits but because people must have faith in their healers. Without faith there can be no magic.

Certain lies may therefore be necessary, if not therapeutic. If lying to a client, deliberately or unintentionally, is unethical since it promotes deceit and deception, perhaps it is just as unethical to be completely truthful (whether it is in the client's best interest or not) just so the therapist can feel pure. Tactical deception, then, has its place in protecting clients from a reality they are not yet prepared to face or in the paradoxical interventions that break stubborn destructive patterns resistant to more conventional attacks. Although lies can be very effective strategies and quite useful in moving progress along, they are not usually one's first choice. No matter how we rationalize the necessity of the lie, whether exaggerating our powers or our confidence, a certain amount of caution, modesty, and uncertainty is very helpful in keeping us from becoming "too big for our britches" or for the client's good. Just because we must tell the client that we know we can help him does not mean we have to believe it, too. But it sure helps.

The Pretense of Perfectionism

Closely related to projecting a false sense of confidence is counterfeit expertise. This occurs when we pretend to know how to do something that we really do not know how to do.

- How many times have you said something you did not understand even if the client pretended he did?
- How many times have you hidden behind a pregnant pause just to give yourself time to figure out where to go next?
- How many times have you heard a client say after a week of reflection: "I finally understood what you were doing last session and what it meant" and had no idea what profound insight you were supposedly developing?
- How many times has a referral contact or colleague or client asked you if you know how to work with a particular disorder, and you replied "Yes," while you scanned your bookshelves for a quick education?
- How many times have you been asked by an inquisitive client what is going on and turned the question back to him until you could make something up?

The pretense of perfectionism may be for the client's benefit, but it affects the therapist as well. If we believed that we really were as thoroughly competent and composed as the image we present to clients, we would be insufferable. Yet if we were continuously honest with ourselves regarding what we know, what we understand, and what we can do, we would be so riddled with self-doubt we could barely function at all. The compromise position is to accept that we exaggerate our capabilities, that such distortion is sometimes necessary for the client's good, but that we should not for a minute forget that we are just pretending. "And if you pretend really well, the people you work with will pretend to make changes. And, they will forget that they are pretending. . . for the rest of their lives. But don't be fooled by it" (Milton Erickson quoted in Bandler and Grinder, 1979, p. 136).

Feeling Indispensable

Any time we act for reasons other than to promote the client's growth we dilute our honesty. This occurs occasionally, especially when we become more familiar with a client we have known for a while. At the same time we are taking care of clients, we take care of ourselves as well. This happens at the invitation of the client or sometimes by our own initiative.

Saying good-bye to a client is so bittersweet that many therapists encounter difficulty in letting go. In most cases letting go represents a successful cure. The client has learned her lessons well, accomplished her goals, obliterated her suffering, and (it is hoped) weaned herself of dependency on the therapist in the process. She feels strong, confident, insightful, and motivated to get on with the rest of her life. She also feels quite grateful to her helper, sad, nervous, and ambivalent about ending this relationship. The therapist shares many of the client's emotions: he feels excited, relieved, and probably confused as well.

Launching a client into the world leaves a vacancy in his schedule and his life. It means a loss of revenue, a disruption in a weekly routine that may have spanned years, and letting go of a dear and trusted friend. Even when it is in the best interest of the client to leave therapy, when the clinician claims to be doing everything in his power to help promote autonomy, his behavior may reveal quite different intentions. After all, keeping a client locked into treatment, with no hope or wish for escape, can ensure a therapist a lifetime income. It is inconvenient to replace a "good" client who knows the rules and does not demand very much for her money.

We all know practitioners who keep their clients addicted to them for decades. They teach people to need them, to require a weekly or daily fix just to function. Of course, some very disturbed people will need therapy throughout their lifetimes just to keep themselves out of the hospital. But here we are referring to those therapists who keep clients long beyond the point where they are doing them any good. One such psychiatrist has been seeing the same twenty clients two to four times per week for decades. His clients are so well heeled (and he is so reluctant to lose income) that when he schedules his annual vacation to the Caribbean he reserves the wing of a motel so that his clients may join him and continue their treatment. It is his opinion, and his clients readily and hysterically agree, that they just cannot function for two weeks without their doctor.

To a lesser extent any clinician in private practice struggles with the issue of when to let clients go. It is easy to say that as long as they keep coming to sessions they must be getting something from the experience. When working for a public agency, the longest I ever saw a client was for fifteen to twenty sessions. At the time I thought I was doing marvelous work. It can hardly have been a coincidence that when I moved into private practice, where my livelihood depended on my ability to keep my schedule full, the average number of sessions I saw a client jumped to forty. I had, naturally, convinced myself that this longer-term approach was much better for the client; it is more intense, more comprehensive, more elegant, more satisfying, more effective, and, yes, more costly.

A psychologist in private practice who is driven toward a goal of financial independence and yet also very dedicated to helping people admits with great discomfort: "I lie when I tell myself I can see thirteen clients in a day and not lose my effectiveness. I hypnotize myself into believing that so I can continue with this ferocious schedule I call my life. Especially I lie whenever I say that I am not doing this kind of work to make a lot of money. Because I am." This is certainly part of what motivates many therapists in private practice — not only to enjoy freedom but to strike it rich. And this attitude affects the pace and style of what we do.

Many things can be said about therapists — that we are knowledgeable, dedicated, compassionate — but we are rarely described as swift in our methods. We take our sweet time in getting to the heart of the matter, embellish our insights with poetry and stories, follow a tortuous route to a client's underlying fears. The lie to clients and ourselves is that we will rid them of their symptoms just as fast as we can. Even a first-year intern knows that if you take away the client's presenting complaints too quickly, he will not stick around for the best part of the show.

Absolutes

A psychology professor reveals: "It's difficult to admit I lie. I can't really think of any . . . well, . . . maybe there's one. I tell my students to have faith in the human capacity for healing. I talk about it as an absolute, but it isn't really. There are a lot of people I don't trust or who can't take care of themselves. Their instincts are all wrong."

There is a tremendous difference between our theories and our actual behavior. To the public, to clients, to colleagues we disclose our neat, coherent little model of why things work the way they do. Most practitioners, with little prodding, can articulate fairly detailed theories about human development, psychopathology, personality development, and psychotherapy. Together with these models of understanding, we also ascribe to specific systems of logic, morality, and epistemology. Finally, we bestow ourselves with titles to summarize the conceptual frameworks to which we owe allegiance: humanist, behaviorist, existentialist, Adlerian, Freudian, Reichian, eclectic. And therein hides the lie.

If the truth were told, most clinicians just do not apply their orthodox theories in their sessions—and for good reasons. Once a person, any person, applies a method invented by someone else, it becomes a different method. Each therapist is simply too individual, with her distinct values, personality, demeanor, and voice, to ever practice therapy the same way another does. Moreover, the interactions with clients force one to think on one's feet, instantaneously, instinctually, no matter what training was received. If we were to stop and think, to reflect on our theories, we would interfere with the smooth flow of action as well as paralyze ourselves with complexity (Schön, 1983). In other words, we do not really function professionally like we say we do, or even like we think we do.

In spite of our labels as social worker or psychologist, counselor or psychiatrist, in spite of our identification with particular theories, we act in accordance with our intuition at the time. Most of the absolutes and rules that we say we follow are used only when appropriate or convenient. The most nondirective of practitioners occasionally gives advice. The most orthodox analyst reveals a distinctly human character. The most rigid rational-emotive therapist will also deal with feelings. And then there are the absolute imperatives of the profession that we all ignore at some time or another.

- *Do not give advice.* We do it all the time when a client is about to do something we feel would be destructive.
- *Do not answer questions.* But we do answer them when we get tired of playing games or when we know the answer and are dying to tell someone.
- *Do not talk about yourself.* Although this may be desirable, it is idealistic and ultimately impossible.
- *Trust the clients' capacity for healing.* If they had sound judgment concerning what is best for them, they would hardly end up in therapy.
- *Do not get involved in your clients' lives.* This is possible only if you sleep through the sessions.

- *You have to like your clients in order to help them.* But for a long time, some of them are genuinely unlikeable.
- *Refer those clients who are beyond your specialties and expertise.* If we did this, we would grow very little and have very few clients.
- *Personality disorders are genuinely untreatable.* But someone has to keep trying.
- *Let the client lead the sessions.* If the client cannot lead his life, how is he going to be in charge of his cure?
- *Protect the confidentiality of the client.* If you do not, you will be vulnerable to a lawsuit.

Myth of Neutrality

One of the foundations of our work is that we are professionals and experts who, like judges or arbitrators, purport to be objective, detached, free of biases and prejudices, and morally neutral. Generations of therapists and clients have been deluded into believing the myth of neutrality in helping—that it is not only desirable but possible to attain. We are cautioned to guard against exposing our true feelings, our prejudices, our convictions, and our values so we do not use unique influence, so we do not impose our morality on others. While those in pastoral counseling make no pretense of disguising their moral agenda, secular practitioners also have a value program of their own. It may be to adopt a particular life-style, a way of thinking or feeling, a political orientation, or a preference toward particular ideas. But basically we want to sell our values of health, risk, honesty, emotional fitness, autonomy, and independence. These are considered "good" values, so they are exempted from the neutrality gag order. But "bad" values like dependence or safety should not be communicated, even if we may sometimes wonder if there is anything so terribly wrong with two people contentedly stuck in a fused, parasitic marriage. There is room for much philosophical debate here—and that is exactly the point. As therapists feel differently about love, marriage, commitment, sexuality, and relationships, so they will work differently in their sessions. Some clients really understand this, so they ignore our lies.

> The phone rings.
> *"Do you do marriage counseling?"*
> *"Yes, I do."*
> *"Are you for or against marriage?"*
> *"That depends on the marriage."*
> *"Let me put it differently. Do most of your couples stay together or get a divorce?"*

Some perceptive clients are right on target with their queries. There are indeed therapists who stress commitment over divorce, sexual affairs over boredom, religion over education, travel over gardening, exercise over television, tea over coffee. We are hardly neutral, even if we try to keep our opinions to ourselves. We have opinions about everything a client says or does. And in the midst of our posture of supposed acceptance, unconditional positive regard, and neutrality, we are sometimes thinking to ourselves: "I wish you wouldn't."

London (1985) believes that, in spite of the myth, therapists are hardly value free, are rarely objective or neutral, and are, in fact, moral agents for their own beliefs. As human beings and members of society, therapists make a number of moral commitments. London points out that moral neutrality is itself a moral position that legitimizes the therapist's preference for freedom, democracy, independence, responsibility, and productivity.

A case could even be made that we ought to be *more* forceful with our values and less morally neutral, or at least do away with much of the pretense. If a suicidal client enters our office, we will do our best to convince him to develop our respect for life. Should a client who lives by her wits, a gambler, a risk taker, a reckless sensation seeker wish our counsel, she will probably get a lecture on living more responsibly. We recommend the books that are most consistent with our life philosophy. In our hearts we believe that what is good for us is good for everyone. Therapists who enjoy traveling urge their clients to travel more. Those who find peace running on a country road or worshipping in a church would probably prefer to have their clients do the same.

If we choose not to impart any particular values, then we will push the big ones—that values are a good thing or that therapy is a marvelous experience that everyone should share. Other essential values espoused by most therapists are clearly articulated by Strupp (1980), Gross and Kahn

(1983), Van Hoose and Kottler (1985), and Corey, Corey, and Callanan (1988). They found that clinicians ranked self-respect, friendships, personal pleasure, individual freedom, and universal love over social or religious institutions. We have a strong bias toward taking responsibility for our thoughts and actions. We bristle at domination, coercion, manipulation. We think insight is a lovely thing, no matter what pain it will bring. In fact, we think pain is just fine, too (especially when it is the psychic kind that belongs to someone else). Even within the client-centered camp there is a movement away from value neutrality. Boy and Pine (1982) suggest that therapists should become more explicit in communicating their values — especially those of free will and a definition of what is good and right.

If we do project our values during our work, what are the personal consequences for client and therapist? We must shoulder the burden not only of relying on our clinical judgment and professional skills but of knowing clients will adopt many of our most personal beliefs. Are we really certain that the way we are living our lives would be all that great for the rest of the world? We can justifiably worry whether it is in anyone's best interest to adopt the values of a typical therapist. Some of our clients come in as just plain folks, naive and sheltered. They may leave enlightened, but at the expense of their innocence.

A Therapist's Personal Skills

The preceding sampling of absolutes that are not strictly followed illustrates the discrepancy between what we say and what we do. These deceptions contribute further to the stress and confusion that therapists experience. Maybe this is our ultimate hypocrisy: while we push clients to expand their potential, strive for greater honesty, and improve their personal effectiveness, we sometimes continue a life of mediocrity. In our offices we are stars—energetic, capable, creative, and powerful. Then we pack up our briefcases and head out into the world, fraudulent heroes.

There is often a major gap between the self our clients come to know and love and the self that we expose to the rest of the world. We are taught to keep our distance from students or clients during accidental social encounters— supposedly to protect them from embarrassment because we have such an intimate knowledge of their lives. But another reason for this distance is to shelter them from the disappointment of finding out we are really quite human. We feel shy and inept. We are not as witty and wise outside our realm. We are threatened by strange situations just like everyone else.

Nevertheless, we are aware of the myth of personal competence we perpetuate. When a client complains of some self-defeating behavior or another, we smile knowingly and ask: "So how can you live with yourself, impaired as you are?" But how many times do we ask a client to master a skill we have not yet mastered or confront a problem that is still unresolved for us? One charismatic therapist reveals his most painful lie.

There is great dissonance between what I ask my clients to do and what I am able to do in my own

*life. In relationships, for example, I encourage peo-
ple to be less defensive in their communication and
more empathetic with their spouse, while I'm aware
in my own life I don't deliver on that stuff at all.
There is a gigantic schism between my personal self
and my much healthier professional self. I struggle
to integrate the two parts of me. If I weren't a
therapist I would do just fine because I would be less
in touch with the ideal self I want to be. But I am a
therapist. I access my ideal self most often when I'm
working. I'm trying very hard to do that more often
when I'm outside my office.*

A therapist is, beyond all else, a fully functioning model for others to emulate, a personally and professionally masterful human being. What are those idealized parts of ourselves we access during work hours but are reluctant or unable to use otherwise? What are the skills and insights we wield so masterfully with clients but somehow forget during personal encounters? Many, many professional skills do carry over to the personal realm. Most therapists, for example, are quite astute at picking up on the vulnerabilities of various people, filing them away, and using them to their advantage at a later time. Therapists are also adept at using their nondefensive confrontation skills or summarizing abilities during normal interactions. But then there are all those things we know how to do, things we do every day, that we do not use as much as we could to enrich the quality of our lives and the lives of those around us.

Focus

When we are receiving monetary compensation for our time, we are more than willing to single-mindedly focus on another person. Through our body posture, eye contact, and other attending behaviors, we communicate our total interest in whatever the client is saying. We hang on every word, note the most subtle nuances of their nonverbal cues, sometimes even take notes on the most inane details of their lives. We always ask pertinent questions and further demonstrate our intense interest by frequently reflecting back to the client what we have heard. All of this is quite wonderful, so much so that a client feels appreciated and understood and is willing to pay lots of money for the privilege.

A few hours later we sit at home talking to our best friend on the phone while doing a crossword puzzle. We absentmindedly listen to our loved ones, the people we prize above our own lives, while glancing through the newspaper, reviewing bills, or simply retreating inside ourselves. The focused interest we are willing to sell we will not give away to the people who matter most.

Compassion

No matter how bizarre or abusive a client becomes, we usually turn the other cheek. With total concern and complete empathy we crawl inside someone else's sandals, boots, or Guccis and feel what she is feeling. Because we fully understand the pain she is experiencing we can be accepting and nondefensive in responding to her anguish. We can duck her anger and diffuse our own frustration in not striking back. A policeman sincerely responds, after wiping the spit off his face from a burly felon he just arrested: "Look, if I've done anything to offend you, I apologize" (Ram Dass & Gorman, 1985, p. 45). The criminal apologizes as well, as people are prone to do when they are treated with compassion.

We feel self-satisfied after such a charitable gesture with a client. We reveal love instead of hate. Then we get into the car to drive home. Someone cuts us off on the freeway, someone with an ax to grind for who knows what reason. We scream obscenities, make rude gestures, and tailgate the offender for three minutes in retribution.

Respect

Unconditional regard and respect for the individual is something we practice effortlessly with a client. We genuinely believe in the intrinsic worth of an individual. We teach the philosophy of respecting other people's rights and dignity, at least during work. How much respect do we genuinely feel for and demonstrate toward the many people we encounter on the street? The wino singing in the alley, the man at the car wash who holds the door and waits for a tip, the kid who will guard your hubcaps for a buck? Gone are the focused interest, the compassion and regard, the respect for each person as a precious being.

Patience

For someone who can sit still in a chair hour after hour, a therapist certainly has a hard time waiting in lines. Probably because we must wait so patiently during work, we are reluctant to do so on our own time. Of all the qualities we must develop, patience is the most difficult: waiting for people to move at their own pace, waiting years sometimes before we can see a noticeable difference in a client's behavior.

Put this expert "waiter" in a room full of people and she will elbow her way to the front, if not to the center of attention, then to the head of the buffet line. A therapist discloses:

> *I really don't understand it. I am so patient in my therapy. I used to practice outwaiting a client during silences just to stay in shape. Now I think my greatest strength as a therapist is to allow my patients to take the time they need. I will sometimes push them, but only after they have taken the initiative. My interpretations are usually subtle and understated. I wait for clients to hear them when they are ready. . . . If not (shrugs), we've got nothing but time. The really strange thing is that people always tell me I make them nervous because I'm always in a hurry. I'm the prototype of a Type A personality. I have only one speed outside of my office — blazing fast. On the phone I refuse to be on hold for more than thirty seconds. That's my rule. I'd rather hang up and do something else. I got in a bad habit of checking my watch during sessions. I time myself going everywhere. People think I am*

the most impatient person alive. Only my patients
know what I'm really like.

Spiritualism

Therapy sessions are packed full of lofty ideals; of mysticism; of higher consciousness; of ontological meaning; of transcendent states; of mind, matter, and oneness with the universe. Therapy works with the three "eyes of the soul": the "eye of flesh," which perceives the external world; the "eye of reason," which categorizes and analyzes data from the senses; and the "eye of contemplation," "by which we rise to a knowledge of transcendent realities" (Wilber, 1983, p. 3). The eye of contemplation is especially relevant to most therapeutic issues, for contained within it is all that is subjective, intuitive, spiritual. The therapist works with a "scope to human existence beyond egoism or personal power" (Hayward, 1984, p. 285). The client is taught not only about his thoughts and feelings and behaviors but about the softness of his heart and the spirit within him. Why, then, if we are so concerned about educating other people's spirits, do we so neglect our own?

Historically, therapists were always poor. They were Buddhist monks, Socratic scholars, priests, wanderers, healers. What they lacked in material affluence they made up for in wisdom and purity of the soul. They felt that to be optimally clear, to understand the nature of all things, to enter someone else's soul, to take away pain, they would first have to leave behind their attachment to the material world.

Only in the last century have therapists attained opulence in addition to (or instead of?) their spiritual power.

Many in the private sector gross six-figure incomes. And those in academia, in public and social service, in agencies and institutions, however meager their salaries, nevertheless stretch their money for all its worth. And now, after working so hard for the money we earn, we feel that we deserve to indulge and entertain ourselves. So our bodies are well fed and our minds are stimulated, but our spirits are under-nourished, longing for the third eye of contemplation that gives meaning to existence.

Self-Control

The self-control of which therapists are capable is obvious. We ignore grumbling stomachs, the urge to yawn, and little voices whining: "Me, take care of *me*." We restrain our impulses to hug, shake, kiss, or strike a client. We sit immobile for hours on end.

How then do we excuse our frequent lack of self-control at home? Gone is the willpower to refrain from overeating. Gone is the ease with which we can hold our temper. Gone is the resolve to stick with an exercise regimen. Where is the self-control that was so much in evidence just hours earlier? We plead exhaustion or a desire to escape from control. Time to relax in front of the television with a bowl of ice cream: "Will you kids shut up and give me some peace!"

There are many other things we do regularly while working that we do not do on our own time. It probably could not be any other way. The lie is not in our inconsistency, not in our laziness and indulgences, but in our perpetuating the myth of our invulnerability. In many ways it is helpful for clients to hold on to this myth. It empowers our role as models. It keeps their attention and stimulates hope. But it also is very confusing for the therapist who must lead a double life, disguising a secret identity.

During a lengthy interview for this book, one therapist was startled by being asked about his lies and self-deceptions. After several minutes of thought he shrugged and said that he really could not think of any self-deceptions that he was aware of. He is a very honest person and, after years in treatment and supervision, he feels very clear and self-aware. I turned off the tape recorder and began to pack up when I heard him clear his throat and whisper: "Everything I've said to you is a lie. It is so important to me to sound and look good that on some level I'm always suspect. I try my hardest and I still can't overcome my need to say and do things other people will approve of. I'm especially an impostor whenever I act like I know what I'm talking about. Even this is a lie."

chapter 8

ALTERNATIVE THERAPIES
FOR THERAPISTS

$\int$ome of the problem areas therapists confront are the predictable result of prolonged practice; some are the result of self-deception and self-destructiveness. These are, of course, in addition to the "normal" cries that every human encounters: the usual variety of personal conflicts, insecurity, mood swings, restlessness, financial pressures, family problems, indecision, stagnation, fears of love, of death, of life. But, unlike the public at large, therapists are well versed in the techniques of avoiding therapeutic experiences — whether these involve counseling ourselves or getting help elsewhere. Those therapists who do make personal growth a major life priority may, in fact, only go through the motions of a cure. For example, the most popular alternative for therapists who seek greater self-awareness and clarity is to undergo a form of psychoanalysis that is part of one's training. Unfortunately, by and large, therapists often make miserable clients. When it comes to changing our own behavior, we are highly skilled at pretense and acting.

A senior psychoanalyst admits: "My biggest lie to myself is when I say I've been psychoanalyzed. Even though I was in analysis for seven and a half years, I was a terrible patient. By no stretch of the imagination could one say it was successful because I refused to allow several important areas of my life to be analyzed. Although I tell people all the time — clients, colleagues — that I've been analyzed, it's just not true. I've got a lot of work left to do."

Whether or not therapists seek enlightenment in the formal contexts of supervision, support groups, or psychotherapy, most are engaged, although not necessarily successfully, in counseling themselves. We just cannot talk to people all day long without hearing a little bit of what we say. We cannot teach people to talk to themselves differently without doing so ourselves.

The Therapist's Developmental Changes

As surely as we know that any client will move through a progression of developmental stages throughout her life, or during the process of therapy, we know that we will experience a series of predictable, sequential, and logical changes during our professional careers. Most therapists begin their vocations from a position of idealism; a loss of innocence often follows. Next comes cynicism and a loss of enthusiasm, followed, one hopes, by pragmatism coupled with realistic expectations, integrated experience, and greater flexibility.

Several critical incidents universally shape a therapist's development, the most obvious of which is the real reason the practitioner entered the field. Usually little similarity exists between the publicly espoused motives (some variation of the theme "to save the world") and the private, perhaps unconscious reasons (some variation of "to save myself"). We all have some hazy personal agenda we have been following since graduate school that responds to an internal force that pushed us into helping others and keeps us there. That agenda may be to simulate the rescuer role that was familiar to us as children or to get therapy for ourselves without having to risk the stigma of seeing a therapist. Becoming a therapist is one way some people seek to fulfill their need for power and control. Others are attracted to the opportunities for having successful relationships with minimum personal involvement. Still others who feel stupid can act wise, those who are selfish can pretend to be altruistic, and people who are timid can be assertive. One therapist relates: "If the truth be known, I couldn't care less about the money and status. I don't spend much anyway. I don't even like working indoors, so it is hardly the comfort factor that keeps me seeing clients. But I do like people being dependent on me. I really do. I get off on being needed. Nobody ever needed me as a kid. I guess because I never had anything that anyone else ever wanted. Now I do. And people will drive long distances, pay money, and jump through hoops for whatever it is I have. I like this feeling. No, I *love* this feeling."

There are both functional and dysfunctional motivators

for entering this profession (Guy, 1987; Kottler & Brown, 1992). On the healthy side of the ledger are attitudes of idealism and altruism; a capacity for and interest in listening to others; intellectual curiosity; a desire for growth; a degree of warmth and compassion; and a tolerance for intimacy, ambiguity, and self-denial. These traits are sometimes balanced by hidden motives that are quite personally and neurotically driven—a desire for power, an interest in using others to work through one's own unresolved issues, unsatiated loneliness and isolation, or even an intention to be exploitive for financial or personal gain.

What are the real reasons you became a therapist? Why do you really stay in the field when it might be much easier to try something else? What are you searching for in books such as this? The answers to these questions will provide the first clues to the critical incidents that shaped and continue to mold our development. These are precisely the areas that may have led us not only into the field but to our own therapy experiences as a client. These will continue to be the same issues we will always counsel ourselves about.

Much of the early therapy training that many of us received occurred growing up in our own families, where we acted as go-betweens, conflict mediators, and helpers. "We kept the peace when our parents argued; we took care of family members who were sick; we helped other family members avoid confronting their pain (Anderson, 1987, p. 19). While this configuration does not apply to every member of our profession, the scenario of being elected to the role of rescuer is a common one.

Previous experiences with therapy are often initial motivators to make the switch from client to helper. Many clinicians can trace their initial interest in the field, as well as their current style of practice, to identification with a therapist who was instrumental in resolving some painful issues. There is a feeling of admiration for this powerful person who understands so much. There are feelings of gratitude and a wish to compensate for this guidance by passing it on to other generations. Since termination issues are never fully worked through, some clients become therapists in order to keep their own therapy going. A student relates: "My parents were so negligent that I was raised by therapists from age fourteen. One after another they all tried to help me, to teach me. Some of them were pretty lousy — they would yell at me and tell me to grow up. Others were fantastic and immensely important. Here I am a grown woman who has been in therapy, on and off, for twenty-five years. I started training as a therapist because I couldn't find anyone left to work with. I figured it was about time I started helping myself — and maybe I could help some others in the process."

The problems that will require the most self-counseling during a therapist's life are those that first appear during the training years. Just as one's motives for entering the field and one's previous experience as a client set the parameters for what one eventually will become, one's graduate education and supervision determine, to a large extent, the more specific forms of one's professional manner. During his apprenticeship, a student undergoes a radical transformation, only a small part of which involves the mastery of theories and skills; most of the changes involve a radical shift in one's thinking and one's self-concept.

During graduate education, the fledgling therapist is exposed to both positive and negative models. If she is unlucky she may even find herself caught in a political tug-of-war between two groups. For self-preservation she will identify with one group or the other. She will find sanctuary under the wing of a mentor and find solace in the books that speak to her. She will work hard to win the approval of her peers and instructors and, in so doing, will create a problem of external control she must counsel herself out of. For the rest of her life she may fight against the bondage created by years of working for grades. No matter how renowned she becomes she may yearn for the external approval she grew addicted to in her youth. She may look to her clients to find out how well she is doing or measure her success by her income or scheduled bookings. But forever she will wrestle with the need for affirmation. This is the gift from her instructors, who taught her to depend on their grades, their evaluations, their commentary, and their approval to know how well she was doing.

Coupled with the need for external validation are the many internal changes a therapist undergoes. There is nothing like having one's hair turn gray, one's stomach turn finicky, or one's memory become unreliable to facilitate a change in life philosophy, values, and therapeutic style. Spending day after day helping others deal with their failing health, decreased vitality, and developmental crises ought to make therapists better prepared to deal with their own. Yet in some ways it is worse since the clinician must live through someone else's mid-life crisis a thousand times. We repeatedly experience, albeit vicariously, menopause and prostate problems. We live through the empty nest syndrome, the launching of adolescents, and the meddling of in-laws more times than we can count. By the time we must face these same problems we are already weary. We know what to expect and still cannot find ways to prevent those common conflicts between parents and children.

Fine (1980) describes a mid-life crisis that afflicts most therapists in the forty-five to fifty-five age bracket: the emergence of despair. This sadness of the soul explored by Chessick (1978) occurs as a result of a therapist's narcissistic vulnerability and prolonged exposure to sickness of the soul, "or, in more mythological terms, the petrification that results from gazing too far, too long, and too deeply at the psychotherapeutic Gorgon's head" (Fine, 1980, p. 393). There is, therefore, an accumulative erosion of will and depletion of spirit that culminates in the mid-life crises well-documented by Erikson (1963) and Levinson (1978). And there are, of course, many other developmental crises to which therapists are hardly immune.

We must counsel ourselves through those endless existential confrontations that "civilians" can easily hide from but therapists must face on a daily basis. When we hear clients confess they sometimes entertain fantasies of jumping off a balcony just for the utter impulse of it, our knees feel weak the next time we look over a railing. Could I jump, too, just for the hell of it? We confront the big issues: death, the fear of going crazy, death, and death again. And always around the corner lies angst, nagging, tugging, tenaciously holding on. Angst is the dread that accompanies a life devoted to enlightenment. Without some form of therapy, it can infect the heart, mind, and spirit, leaving the victim in a state of permanent disillusionment.

Therapist's Resistance and Hypocrisy

There is a marked reluctance on the part of many therapists to seek therapy for themselves. In one survey of practitioners' attitudes toward the value of their craft for resolving their own problems a full one-third stated that whereas they might consult with family, friends, or colleagues, they would not see a therapist (Deutsch, 1985). Just like so many clients we see, many of them believed that asking for help was a sign of weakness or failure.

For a group of people who spend their whole lives engaged in the practice of helping, we seem to exhibit a lot of resistance to getting it for ourselves. Several therapists who were interviewed for this book declined to comment on their method of working through their own problems. Just before abruptly terminating the interview, one respondent typified the hostility and defensiveness this issue arouses:

"You ask me what I do when I encounter personal problems. One thing I would never do is see another therapist. I might try to work it through myself first, and then talk to my wife, but I would *never* go to anyone else. I just don't trust other professionals. And even if I did, I've never had a reason to go. "

Although this response is not typical of our profession, it occurred often enough to merit closer inspection. We may not all be as rigid, threatened, and mistrustful as this particular therapist, but many of us do seem to feel that therapy is for others. No less than a dozen therapists responded to the questions about personal problems with a simple: "I can't think of any."

At first I wondered whether there might really be some among us who have attained a state of nirvana, perfect specimens of emotional and behavioral functioning who have transcended the problems of mortal beings. More than likely, questions that ask therapists to look at their vulnerabilities elicit the same kind of reactions as they would in a client. We deny we have problems. Those we grudgingly admit to, we think we can handle ourselves. We become defensive and irritable; we prefer our illusions of grandeur.

This resistance to examining ourselves with the same critical, diagnostic eye that we would direct toward a client amounts to utter hypocrisy. If we do not genuinely believe that the therapeutic tools of our profession can work on us, we have no business practicing them on anyone else.

Some Therapists Speak for Themselves

In addition to entering formal psychotherapy, there are a number of alternative methods that clinicians might use to pursue their own growth. A sampling of voices follows.

"*My therapy is to do therapy. Being myself with my clients. I need a certain amount of contact with other people or I would stay alone. My clients affirm me, they challenge me, they push me to keep up with them.*"

"*I get together with a colleague on a regularly scheduled basis and we take turns being in the role of client and therapist with one another. As long as I can schedule my crises for the week when it is my turn to be the client, everything works out fine.*"

"*My therapy is talking with my wife. Sharing with her my fears. Opening myself up to her feedback. I think self-disclosing wherever and whenever I can is therapeutic for me. Telling people when I'm afraid. Forcing myself to be honest about what I'm feeling.*"

"*I travel a lot as a way to energize myself. When I'm away on a trip I don't even think about my children, much less my clients. I don't know how I do it, but I do. Once I'm on the way to the airport I let go of everything. The geographic distance creates a psychological distance. I shed my skin as a therapist and become a person in movement.*"

"*I'm so damn driven and ambitious I had to find a way to slow myself down. I needed to do some-*

thing just for myself—not for an audience, not for my resume, not even for a sense of accomplishment. That's why I've been playing the guitar for two years and nobody has ever heard me. When I concentrate on the music I can't possibly think about anything else. For a few minutes nothing exists except my breathing, my fingers, the sounds I hear and feel."

"It started out that running was to be my therapy. It helped me sleep at night, forget my troubles, and do something nice for myself. Then I became obsessed and the cure became the problem. I developed knee and hip problems while training for marathons. After a while I approached running like I do everything else: I became competitive and regimented. It was no longer an escape but another obligation. Now I'm down to just a few miles a day and it helps a lot to keep myself centered."

"My therapy is gardening and digging in the dirt and watching things grow. My therapy is playing golf. My therapy is doing crossword puzzles. My therapy is being with friends, entertaining, going out. And sometimes my therapy is just doing nothing, just nothing at all."

"Being a therapist helps me to question myself a lot, to ask myself what I need. When I can feel a

knot inside me, I know it's time to go work out or
just get under the covers for a while."

"My husband is a wonderful help to me. He is
very sensitive to me. He can sense what I need even
before I do. He knows when I want to be hugged or
when I want to be taken care of. I've been taking
care of people all day long, so when I get home I
need time to let go."

"I live by certain rules. I never see more than
eight clients in a day. I try not to see two appoint-
ments back to back. I spread them out over the week
and leave deliberate holes during the middle of the
day to feed myself, replenish myself. I read, go for
walks, talk to friends during breaks. My therapy is
in just the way I schedule myself so I don't feel
overburdened."

These samples of therapeutic alternatives set the tone
for what is possible in self-nourishment for professional
helpers.

Self-Therapy

Each of the following self-administered therapies that will
be reviewed is a further example of what clinicians often
do to keep themselves emotionally fit and spiritually
energized.

When Therapists Talk to Themselves

There are many ways a therapist works to counteract angst and manage the transformations that are part of the helping life-style. Talking to ourselves as we would to clients is the most direct and effective cure. This self-administered therapy is especially advantageous in those situations in which we may be needlessly worrying about clients or having difficulty separating ourselves from others. If we find, during odd moments of the day or while tossing in bed, that we are unable to let go of our work, we may initiate a self-dialogue such as the following: "How am I helping my clients by spending time worrying about their welfare? If I'm not helping them, then what is this behavior doing for me? Inflating my sense of importance? Using magical thinking to prevent tragedy by anticipating it? Distracting myself from something in me?"

Consistent with but not restricted to the tenets of rational-emotive or cognitive-behavioral therapy is the suggestion that therapists use self-talk to dispute their irrational strivings for success and perfection (Ellis, 1984). On a broader scale, those confrontations, interpretations, and challenges that produce the most dramatic impact on a client's behavior will do the same for us. After all, we are experts at talking people out of their suffering. We give pep talks that motivate clients to overcome their fears. We convincingly challenge them to let go of beliefs that are not helpful. We teach clients to talk to themselves so that they can carry our voices with them wherever they may go. At times when they balk or stutter, our words of encouragement come back to them. We repeat our favorite strategies of self-talk so often that they have become our personal prayers. During moments of stress or difficulty, they return to haunt us. There is nothing as uncomfortable for a therapist as catching himself feeling self-pity and hearing his own words in his mind, echoing exactly what he would say to a client in a similar situation.

It is through the testing of a particular intervention on ourselves that we first discover its possible utility in a session. A therapist who is gnashing his teeth in frustration over a difficult client notices that he calms down considerably when he reminds himself: "This is what I'm paid to do." Not only does this self-talk help him to calm down, but later, with the same client, he is able to urge the use of this identical strategy: "You get so angry at the customers for complaining about their purchases, so instead you transfer your hostility to me. But what do you expect to hear while working in public relations? Customers are supposed to yell at you. So every time you let their whining get to you, just remember: their job is to complain; yours is to listen without feeling defensive."

We are constantly telling people how to talk to themselves. An adolescent mourning the loss of his girlfriend is instructed to tell himself his pain is necessary and a sign of how much love he is capable of feeling. A woman straddling the line just this side of panic is urged to tell herself the impending attacks will subside if she will remind herself of where she is and what is really happening around her. An obese man is cautioned that every time he reaches for food he does not need he should tell himself he is hiding from his pain. By teaching others to counsel themselves at will, the therapist internalizes the same therapeutic messages.

We may find it necessary to counsel ourselves in the same situations in which we recommend that clients use self-talk.

- When we feel uncomfortable in social situations ("What have I really got to lose by approaching these people?")
- When the car will not start ("Getting mad right now is *not* going to start the car.")
- When we are about to lose our temper ("This just isn't all that important.")
- When we do not get what we want ("Oh, well.")
- When we are about to do something that might get us in a lot of trouble ("Is is worth it, and if so, am I willing to pay the price of getting caught?")

There are also a number of instances in which the use of self-talk strategies are particularly helpful in a therapist's life.

- When a client becomes worse after our intervention ("I guess this means I'm not perfect and the client isn't yet ready to change. Time to try Plan B.")
- When one's mind drifts elsewhere during a session ("Concentrate, concentrate.")

- When a client will not talk during a session ("Just relax. Take a deep breath. He'll talk when he has something to say.")
- When a client fails to show up for an appointment ("Don't take it personally. Getting mad isn't going to help the client, and it surely isn't going to help me. What can I do with my time instead?")
- When a session is interrupted by someone knocking at the door ("No big deal. Let me just deal with this and then get back to work.")
- When a client does not pay his bill ("What an annoyance. How can I take care of this so that I won't have to think about it anymore?")
- When there is not enough work to do ("I guess it's time to hustle up some work. Things are always slow this time of year.")
- When there is too much work to do ("The world isn't going to end just because I don't finish all of this stuff today.")
- When a client becomes abusive ("Oops. I'm letting him get to me.")
- When we feel blocked with a client ("What is getting in the way of my being helpful?")
- When in spite of our best efforts the client does not improve ("I can't reach everybody all of the time.")

When we listen to our own interventions and apply them to ourselves during self-dialogues, we demonstrate the true effectiveness of what we teach. After having said these things to ourselves and noted the results, we have greater conviction in what we say to clients. Again we note the interaction between the personal and the professional in a therapist's life. As we stumble across some way of expressing a motivational or insightful idea during a session, we rub our hands in glee knowing we can use it again and again with other clients and especially with ourselves. And when we encounter a particularly poetic expression during social conversations, while watching a movie, or while walking in the woods, we smile inwardly and store it away for later use.

When Therapists Solve Their Own Problems

A second set of strategies for therapist self-counseling involves treating ourselves as we would our clients by using our capacity for healing, nourishment, insight, and motivation to enrich our lives. This can range from simply noting our defensiveness in a threatening situation to designing an elaborate problem-solving package including short- and long-term goals, contingencies, reinforcements, and action strategies. By applying our therapeutic wisdom and skills to ourselves, we increase our personal effectiveness as we field-test our best interventions on our most severe critic.

Those practitioners who are behaviorally inclined have an incredibly wide range of techniques at their disposal to help in defining and solving problems. Even therapists who work primarily with insight and deplore systematic training in decision making are nevertheless quite skilled at helping people get to the bottom of what is bothering them and then remedy the situation. Whether we teach problem-solving skills directly or by combining them with other interventions, we are experts at understanding how and why problems develop and what can be done to solve them, or at least to live with them.

One psychologist feels especially successful at being his own best client when it comes to applying his problem-solving system to himself: "I am constantly applying to myself the model that I use with my clients. I try to define the problem I'm experiencing in specific operational terms. I look at the precipitating and contributing factors, the intervening variables, and why the problem continues to exist. I create a plan based on what I want and what needs to be done."

No other professional in any field works so intimately with the process of constructive thinking. As applied philosophers we not only understand the intricacies of logic, ethics, metaphysics, and epistemology, but we are readily able to employ their methodologies in solving everyday problems. We teach people how to think more rationally, to feel more appropriately, to behave more constructively. We can sort out the complexities of that chaos we call emotional disturbance. We know how to simplify the salient issues, shelve the distractions, and focus in on the core issues. We are experts at ranking priorities in terms of their pertinence to desired goals. We can juggle the different loose ends while we determinedly push forward with a plan of action, then return to any number of related themes that were left hanging.

We are not only masters of deductive and inductive

reasoning, practical philosophers who can cut through the gristle to the real meat of an issue, but scientists by training and inclination. We use empirical methodologies to objectively evaluate the effects of any variable or intervention. We test hypotheses in our sessions with deceptive precision. We systematically collect the data that are pertinent to a particular case, isolate the dependent variables, and then, with flexibility and stubbornness, try out any number of treatment variables while scrutinizing their impact on the client, on ourselves, on the flow and movement of the sessions.

That we can integrate so many skills and diverse bodies of knowledge into a coherent system of problem solving is testimony to our potential for an ideally healthful existence. The hard part is applying all that we can do to help clients solve their problems to the resolution of our own issues. Even with our defenses and subjectivity, with the limitations involved in using oneself as an object of self-study, we can certainly accomplish more than we presently do.

The voice of a social worker: "I was stuck in my job and couldn't see a way out. I had talked to a friend, even tried therapy myself for a while, but nothing much changed except that I developed even stronger excuses and better rationalizations for avoiding change. Sometimes I hate being a therapist for just that reason. Why can't I be more innocent and trusting—just let things happen instead of analyzing everything? Anyway, for a long time I gave up. I thought I had tried everything I knew how but was a failure as my own client—or anyone else's for that matter. But then I just let go. I'd done that lots of times before with clients.

When they fight back or become defensive, I just let go. I tell them to keep their misery if they like it so much; they're just not ready yet to change. When I told a client that again for the fortieth time last month it occurred to me I could do that with myself, too. I did. And that's how I ended up in my new job."

Journal Keeping

A number of painfully introspective writers, including Anaïs Nin, John Steinbeck, Thomas Wolfe, Andre Gide, and Albert Camus, kept journals throughout their lives as a way to maintain their sanity and clarity after pouring out so much of themselves in their work. Carl Jung was the first to recognize the merits of the diary for a practicing therapist. It was in his Black Book that he first developed his theories; analyzed his dreams, fantasies, and symbols; recorded the events of his life; and conducted imaginary dialogues with his unconscious. Rainer (1978) found Jung's example inspirational, particularly when merged with the creative self-therapy approach of Anaïs Nin, who devoted her life to exploring psychological themes as a woman, a therapist, and a writer. Jung opened a door that other clinicians were able to open even wider.

> *Although Jung used the journal as a vehicle for a heroic journey into the sea of the unconscious, he concluded that an awareness of dreams and inner images always needs to be integrated with the pragmatic realities of every day existence: "Particularly at*

this time, when I was working on the fantasies, I
needed a point of support in 'this world.' It was
most essential for me to have a normal life in the
real world as a counterpoise to the strange inner
world" [Jung quoted in Rainer, 1978, p. 22].

Writing letters to colleagues and friends can also be a form of self-therapy and catharsis for the therapist struggling with new ideas and insights or with his personal pain. Freud began his five-year correspondence with his best friend Wilhelm Fleiss to explore his burgeoning theories and to promote his self-analysis. He did the same with trusted colleagues such as Jung. These early pioneers quickly discovered that in the role of confidant to others a structure must be created for the therapist to become a confidant to himself. Systematic journal writing serves just that function for therapists in several different ways (Dyer & Vriend, 1977; Kottler, 1983).

1. *It is a way to supervise oneself and work through difficulties with particular cases.* It could be said that all client resistance results, in part, from some blocking that occurs in the therapist. The journal provides a vehicle to explore the dynamics of being stuck with a client. We can examine our feelings and thoughts as they are elicited by a session's content. We can keep track systematically of the interventions we use with clients in given situations and note their specific effects. We can also outline in writing the facts and impressions of a case so as to structure alternative treatment plans.

The journal is useful for a therapist in following the patterns of his professional behavior over time. When we encounter a client with concerns similar to those we have worked with successfully or unsuccessfully before, we can review the interventions we tried before to avoid repeating mistakes. Naturally, journal writing is the single most helpful structure for working through feelings of counter-transference with clients.

2. *It is a method of self-analysis.* Freud's need to pour out his feelings accelerated during the period of his greatest introspection: "My own analysis is going on, and it remains my chief interest. Everything is still dark, including even the nature of the problems, but at the same time I have a reassuring feeling that one only has to put one's hand in one's own store-cupboard to be able to extract—in its own good time—what one needs" (Freud, [1897] 1954, p. 227).

Extracting what one needs becomes a much simpler task if there is some repository where things are stored. The journal becomes for the therapist a place to pour out his heart. It is the place for exploring one's hidden motives, unconscious desires, and unresolved struggles. It is the place for catharsis and free association, where dreams are expressed and analyzed, where the structure and patterns of one's life become evident.

3. *It is a vehicle for developing and recording ideas.* Many novelists have used their journals to create intricate plots, sketch their characters, or record ideas they may someday use. In his journal, Thomas Wolfe processed the work of his predecessors and scrupulously considered his

contemporaries, attempting to define for himself the nucleus of all he would later write about: "Literature is, in any sense, a criticism of life. That criticism is either actual or implied. Especially does this hold true of drama. If we really desire literature, the artist must be given full scope in which to exercise his talent. . . . Any attempt to make him the creature of public squeamishness will kill him and his art. If we are not willing to meet these conditions, we are not ready for the art; we are not worthy of literature" (Kennedy & Reeves, [1921] 1970, p. 7).

All therapists are theoreticians. We harbor our own unique ideas about how the world works and how therapy ought to be conducted. No matter what school of thought we align ourselves with, we have our own individual notions about how best to work. The journal is the best place to articulate these ideas, to formulate our theories, and to grow as thinking beings.

4. *It is a record of significant events.* Therapists are more aware than most of the value in studying one's past in order to make sense of the present and future. By reviewing the history of a client's developmental growth and studying the critical incidents in a client's life, we come to discover what is creating the present complaint. Our journal allows us to do this for ourselves.

There are milestones worth recording in everyone's life: births, deaths, job changes, the loss of innocence, successes, and failures. Journal keeping helps us maintain our perspective on where we have been and where we are going. It is a way to remember things we have experienced. And, best of all, it becomes a structure for committing ourselves to future goals. As we work toward these goals and counsel ourselves in the process, we become more personally and professionally effective.

Exercise

Because therapists do their work in a chair, using their intellects and voices, many find relief exercising the body. While the mind remains active through its diagnostic and reasoning chores, the body remains inert, wasting away in some places and growing in others through neglect.

That therapists have jumped on the physical exercise bandwagon is not surprising. We who understand that total wellness requires the interaction of mind and body, who observe at close range how a sick brain can destroy a healthy body and how failing health can sap one's will, feel committed to the nourishment of our total being. Whether the activity is intended primarily for aerobic conditioning, esthetics, entertainment, rehabilitation, or distraction, a regular exercise program serves a therapist's needs. The reasons for beginning such a program can be as varied as those for the population at large.

- To prolong life
- To increase self-discipline
- To serve as a self-medication for stress
- To improve esteem and confidence
- To make oneself more attractive
- For body cathexsis

- To sleep better
- To control weight

But therapists also have other reasons to exercise: to engage in something nonverbal, to give oneself silent time in an enlightened state — time for processing the day, for calming down, for beginning or ending a day of confronting other people's troubles.

When I ride my bike the wind washes me clean. Everything I have soaked in during the previous days oozes out through my pores, all the complaints and pain and pressure. I feel only the pain in my legs and lungs as I climb up a hill pumping furiously. And then I coast down as fast as I can, never knowing what is around the next turn. For an hour or two I am no longer a receptacle for other people to dump their suffering. Nobody catches me on my bike. There is no time to think or I will miss a pothole in the road. And it takes too much concentration watching for traffic, pacing my rhythm, switching gears, working on technique, saving my strength, breathing slowly to consider anything outside my body. After a ride through the country, I feel ready again to face my clients, my past, and my uncertain future.

Group Support

In addition to attempting some form of self-therapy to promote serenity and enlightenment, a number of changes can be initiated to make life easier yet more stimulating. Maslach (1982), for example, suggests the use of group ritual for therapist nourishment. If certain rules can be imposed to severely curtail endless complaints or criticism (such as what occurs in many teachers' lounges), informal groups can provide a special source of energy. Moss (1981) finds the group to be a tremendous healing force for therapists in that there is a sense of sharing and of community; the embracing of relationships; and a universal, dynamic, and focused energy that everyone may draw inside his or her being. This is, of course, in addition to the usual transformational powers of a group through the dynamics of cohesion and intimacy. Moss feels that certain key elements should be part of such a transformational group: several multidimensionally awakened people; a setting that is conducive to an inspired process; commitment on the part of participants to release old patterns, to trust, and to be together; the infusion of love; and grace.

Such support groups, in some shape or form, spring up spontaneously in organizations. A room, a tree, or a bench may be designated as an informal gathering place where clinicians can meet during breaks or between sessions. This sanctuary is a place to get a back rub or to talk about cases. It is a safe place to unload and release the negative energy that has accumulated during previous sessions. Therapists who work in isolation often organize a weekly meeting of minds and hearts outside of their offices.

Friends and family supply a comparable source of support for many therapists. We all need a place we can go to cleanse ourselves, to talk through our concerns, and to get our mental and emotional functioning tuned up.

Even with regular therapy and supervision, a clinician still needs daily support. This is often accomplished through debriefings at the end of the day with one's spouse, with a special friend, or with colleagues. As one clinician reports: "Even when I was seeing a therapist once a week and paying for supervision twice a week I still felt the need for something else. Talking to my wife every night and a psychiatrist friend occasionally took some pressure off, but not enough. That's when I started roping some colleagues to join me for informal gatherings during the day. Whereas previously we had bitched together a lot — about the paperwork, Blue Cross, or some departed associate — I began asking them for help. Pretty soon we were all focused on the problems we were having and what we could do about them. It became not so much a therapy group as a bunch of people who were open to whatever happened."

In a support group for therapists, each participant presents a different nuance on the theme of professional depletion. Tanya works experientially with her clients and thus opens herself up to what Mahrer (1989) describes as understanding clients' worlds by accessing her own inner feelings. This highly personal and intuitive style is quite effective for her work, but she pays a dear price in being unable to fully metabolize and dissipate the pain and suffering she encounters. She comes to the meetings each week in order to lance the wounds that have been festering inside her — the client she committed involuntarily to the hospital who screamed accusations of betrayal as she was carried into the ambulance; another client, a young child, who is the victim of satanic rituals but who is unable, as yet, to deal with the extent of his trauma.

Kevin mediates a lot of custody disputes. No matter which party he decides in favor of, or what recommendations he makes, somebody is always very upset with his choice. Whereas he must appear before judges, attorneys, and colleagues as a paragon of confidence in his reports, inside he is wracked with doubts. Did he do the right thing? Who lied to him? Should he change his mind? Could he have done a more thorough job?

Kevin needs to tell someone, preferably a group of peers, about his doubts. The support group helps him come to terms with the realization that no matter how much he studies, how hard he works, how experienced he becomes, he will still never meet his own expectations of perfection.

Fred comes to the group for input on cases, he says. Maybe the others can think of something he might have missed. They do. Every client he struggles with presents issues quite similar to those he has not fully resolved. His habit of giving clients advice and recommending books for them to read is based less on their needs than on his feelings of inadequacy, his belief that as a therapist he is not really doing anything.

Paula recently noticed that she has become seductive with her male clients. She was bewildered by the number of men who had "fallen in love" with her, until group members pointed out that it probably was not a coincidence that this rash of lovestruck clients had occurred about the same time her own divorce proceedings began.

Debbie has no specific personal issue she is working on; she comes to the group for a "tune up" — a sort of preventive maintenance to help keep her balanced. Ron also feels that things are going quite well in his life, both personally and professionally; but he knows, based on his past experience, that he cannot do this type of intense work, get close to others' maelstroms of pain, without occasionally getting singed.

On a more informal basis, several therapists from different agencies commit themselves to meeting for lunch every Friday. During the first few months they spoke only about cases they were stuck with or complained about their respective administrative staffs. Then they made a rule that they would limit their lunch discussion to subjects that would revitalize one another, focusing on encouraging each other to be more creative and innovative.

Adventure and Escape

One final form of therapy many practitioners use to reinvigorate themselves is vicarious or actual adventure. Camping out in front of the television for an evening or losing oneself in a two-hour movie is a wonderful way to turn off one's brain, sit passively, and allow other people to provide the entertainment. Escape fiction is an even better option since books take longer to get through and the "treatment" can be self-administered as needed. I would expect that John D. MacDonald, Elmore Leonard, Robert Parker, Law-

rence Sanders, and Robert Ludlum have rescued more than
one therapist from boredom or despair.

Many enjoy more active forms of adventure and escape
in travel. Away from the office, our homes, our clients, and
our colleagues, we regain a perspective on what is important. Eventually there comes a time when we grow tired of
living out of a suitcase and feel ready, if not eager, to return
to that which we call work.

Any of the alternative therapies covered in this chapter
or any of the other creative endeavors in the one that follows
can serve as a means of escape, of detachment from the
therapist's role. Our reservoir of energy is slowly depleted
with every session we conduct until replenishment becomes
a necessity rather than a choice. Whether the individual
practitioner finds peace in a church or synagogue, in a
theater, in a garden, in a sports arena, or on the road is
beside the point. The important thing is to do something
for ourselves so that we can take things less personally, lower
our expectations to realistic levels, break away as we need it,
and talk to ourselves as we do to our clients. Most of all, by
doing something for ourselves we demonstrate that we take
our own growth just as seriously as we do the growth of those
who buy our services.

chapter 9

TOWARD CREATIVITY
AND PERSONAL GROWTH

*t*here are some writers who believe that therapy, as a profession, could quite legitimately be housed in an academy of dramatic arts instead of a school of education, social work, medicine, or liberal arts. "In this setting, therapists would speak of their craft as professional conversation, strategic rhetoric, or even a genre of interactional theater" (Keeney, 1991, p. 1).

Treating the practice of therapy as a creative art certainly has as much merit as viewing it as applied science. If science is its brain, creativity is the heart of therapy. It is the source of our intuition, the flexibility that leads to innovative models, and the energy that drives our most inspired inventions. Creativity is the essence of what makes each one of us so uniquely powerful and influential.

Therapists must be creative because so much of what we do is spontaneous and improvisational, reacting and responding in the moment to whatever is happening. We are creative in the ways we organize our knowledge and research base so that we can retrieve stuff on demand. We are creative in the ways we frame and understand client issues, in the ways we modify and refine our clinical style, and certainly in the methods by which we deal with impasses that inevitably occur. Creativity also plays a role in the ways we maintain a freshness in our perspective, in the ways we stay energized and continue growing, learning, and improving our effectiveness. Finally, we are creative in the sometimes ingenious ways we help clients to break loose from their rigid, self-defeating patterns, to think, feel, and act differently.

Everything comes together for a therapist in the creative process. Boredom, burnout, and other professional hazards are neutralized when we experience a major insight. Through an innovative procedure, we share our passion for discovery with the client.

The creative journey toward a new understanding, for the client or the therapist, follows a progression from the familiar to the unknown. During this passage there is a move from stable ground to confusion, frustration, self-doubt. To be successful in creative endeavors requires abandoning the verbal and the concrete for the uncertainties of intuition and subjectivity. Despite the risks implicit in any creative endeavor, a therapist has little choice but to continue the natural evolution toward personal and professional growth.

The Urge to Create

Therapists are, at least theoretically, self-actualizing people. Maslow (1968) eloquently connected this intrinsic growth motive with the urge to create. He described one of his subjects, a psychiatrist and pure clinician who had little use for research or theory, as follows: "This man approached each patient as if he were the only one in the world, without jargon, expectations, or presuppositions, with innocence and naiveté and yet with great wisdom, in a Taoist fashion. Each patient was a unique human being and therefore a completely new problem to be understood and solved in a completely novel way" (p. 136).

Personal growth and creativity are synonymous in the life of a therapist. The very process of therapy "involves the elucidation and creation of different patterns of meaning" (Hobson, 1985, p. 108). Ideally it is possible to use our creative thinking for the benefit of enlightenment. We do this in our offices as well as at home. A child therapist works in solo practice but never feels lonely or isolated; instead she finds the solitude more conducive to trying things her own way: "At first I thought I don't really do much that is creative. I mean I don't write or anything like that. But I do many things that are indeed unusual. The way I do therapy always changes. I use art or music or movement or anything that strikes me at the time in my sessions. I trust that aspect of myself. I think the way that I live is creative. I have a great sense of humor. I *do* a lot of creative things. There have been times I've awakened the kids at 2:00 A.M. to drive downtown for ice cream. Or sometimes I like to do crazy things like hide from my husband when he comes home from work and then jump out and scare him."

The creative urge in therapists is ignited not only by the challenge of a client's problem but by a person who "looks on the world as fit for change and on himself as an instrument for change" (Bronowski, 1978, p. 123). Much of our existence is defined by the ways we can leave the world different after we are gone.

Why do we experience the urge to create, if not "to reach beyond our own death" (May, 1975, p. 17)? On the simplest level, the most basic of all human drives is to create another life in our own image, to perpetuate our gene pool. Our survival as a species has depended not only on the persistence of our progeny but on our ability as versatile, cunning, and creative problem solvers (Breuer, 1982).

Therapists have more than their share of creative energy. Our ideas live for generations through every client we help. People may forget their grocer or their fourth-grade teacher or their neighbor, but they never forget their therapist. What a client will remember about his therapist is likely to be a particularly novel idea she introduced to him or a familiar concept that was presented in an instructive way. For this reason, a therapist will live as long as her ideas survive.

Resistance to Creativity

On first sight, creative acts are often viewed as a form of deviance. A brief glimpse into our field's history reveals a number of contributions that were initially scorned and ridiculed. Neither Freud nor anyone who has come on the scene since has had an easy time finding a sympathetic audience for his or her radical approaches to helping.

People are threatened by new ideas that challenge what they think they already know. Resistance to creative thinking is much more the norm than the exception. Especially in the evolution of science, professional thinkers have much preferred esthetics and symmetry in their ideas to the chaos of reality. Boorstein (1983, p. 86) comments on why it took so long for explorers, who long had the necessary technology, to find and plot the geographical world: "The great obstacle to discovering the shape of the earth, the continents, and the ocean was not ignorance but the illusion of knowledge. Imagination drew in bold strokes, instantly serving hopes and fears, while knowledge advanced by slow increments and contradictory witnesses. Villagers who themselves feared to ascend the mountaintops located their departed ones on the impenetrable heavenly heights."

One scientist who sought to climb the mountain and find out for himself why so many people depart life before their time was Ignay Semmelweiss. Koestler (1964) mentions his case as an example of the inevitable and stubborn resistance that accompanies any creative act that revolutionizes our thinking. In 1847 Semmelweiss discovered that it was the filth, bacteria, and residual cadaveric material on a surgeon's hands that caused infections in patients who became worse after operations. "As an assistant at the General Hospital in Vienna, Semmelweiss introduced the strict rule of washing hands in chlorinated lime water before entering the ward. Prior to this innovation one out of every eight women in the ward had died of puerperal fever; immediately afterward mortality fell to one in thirty, and the next year to one in a hundred. Semmelweiss's reward was to be hounded out of Vienna by the medical profession—which was moved, apart from stupidity, by resentment of the suggestion that they might be carrying death on their hands. He went to Budapest but made little headway with his doctrine, denounced his opponents as murderers, became raving mad, was put into a restraining jacket, and died in a mental hospital" (pp. 239–240).

A similar but less dramatic fate of ostracism befell many other creative geniuses—Copernicus, Galileo, Darwin, Mozart, van Gogh, to name but a few representatives of their fields. In most cases a creative idea is first viewed with suspicion and resentment. Perhaps this probationary period is constructive in that it filters out many worthless eccentricities; innovators who can stand the test of time and the criticism of their peers endure.

Creativity is often resisted in therapy because it usually involves breaking rules. Our culture may endorse the idea of creativity, but it certainly does not embrace new structures that render the old ones obsolete. Bloom (1975) mentions how creative acts within our field often stand in opposition to the structures that were built by those currently in power. Inevitably there will be tension and conflict before the new ideas can be accepted. When breaking rules for the sake of finding successful, novel solutions to client problems, Bloom suggests remembering the following points.

1. All rules eventually will be broken.
2. Be prepared to face the consequences (tension and wrath) after introducing a new idea.

3. Compare the effectiveness of old and new before making a public pronouncement.
4. Assume that every client deserves to be treated as a unique and individual challenge that deserves a creative solution.
5. Not all creative ideas are good ideas. Some are not practical, some are not useful, and others are downright dangerous in that they could harm more people than they could ever help.
6. Creativity involves taking risks.

Risking and Creativity

The mentality of the beginner in this profession is to avoid creative or risky behavior for fear of harming somebody. The mid-career professional may avoid creative or risky activities in favor of what is tried and true (Millon, Millon, & Antoni, 1986). In both instances, the clinician is locked into a safe, predictable style of working that will produce consistent if unremarkable results.

Risk and fear are synonymous. There cannot be the possibility of gain without the possibility of loss — no matter how carefully one anticipates and prepares. Taking risks means, to some, the possibility of making the wrong choice. In almost all cases it means breaking the status quo.

Creative acts are risky because they deal with unknown consequences. For this reason the tightrope walker Philipe Petit, who danced on a cable suspended between the two tallest buildings in the world, laughed at being called a risk taker: "I have no room in my life for risk. You can't be both a risk taker and a wirewalker. I take absolutely no risks. I plan everything the most that I can. I put together with the utmost care that part of my life" (Keyes, 1985, p. 10).

The risk in trying something new in therapy is that it is possible, if not probable, that it will not work in the first several attempts. We risk losing our way and becoming lost.

The process of doing therapy awakens in us the sense of ourselves as explorers. We teach others to discover uncharted territory, to learn survival skills and apply them in conditions of maximum stress. We teach people about their limits and their capabilities. We help people take controlled risks where much of the danger can be anticipated.

Risk — the possibility of failure or loss — cannot be avoided if the possibility of success is to have any meaning. There are risks of emotion that involve honestly and spontaneously expressing feelings, admitting fear, or professing love. There are risks of growth in giving up control, in being yourself, or in trying something that has never been attempted before. There are risks of intimacy in working through vulnerability, jealousy, and trust. There are risks of autonomy in cutting off dependencies and being more responsible. And there are risks of change that involve breaking old rules, patterns, and habits and moving into the world of the unknown (Viscott, 1977).

Norcross and Guy (1989) noted that those practitioners who are most satisfied with their work are those who do not have to do it full time. This includes academics, administrators, and teachers who have part-time practices. They enjoy the freedom of choosing whom they will see and when they will see them. Most professionals do not have that choice even if they do exert some control over the professional tasks they perform — whether that includes a blending of administrative, supervisory, and clinical duties; a balance of outreach, paperwork, the therapy; or a combination of individual, family, and group work. Joy in this, or in any work, comes from the experience of freedom to pursue what one most enjoys in ways best suited to one's preferences and style.

Creative Problem Solving

Some of the best examples of creative problem solving come from the family therapy practitioners, who seek to break rigid hierarchies of power and vicious cycles designed to repel any outside intervention. Innovation and experimentation are the hallmarks of these strategic helpers, who rely on strange, novel, sometimes hilarious means to initiate change in difficult clients. In describing the methodologies of famed healer Milton Erickson, Haley (1973) recited a litany of radical and seemingly ridiculous cures that involved prescribing the symptoms, encouraging resistance or a relapse, or telling apparently distracting stories. Haley (1987, 1989) developed even further the concept of creative problem solving in his own brand of ordeal therapy, which seeks unusual ways of changing behavior by presenting to the client an alternative that is even less desirable than his symptoms. In this form of helping, the therapist is encouraged to think outside the usual parameters of our field. The lesson in this is certainly not that we should all be practicing this often bizarre form of treatment, which has its own problems in downplaying the client's responsibility in the process, minimizing the value of insight, and deliberately perpetuating more mystery and manipulation than is probably needed. Rather, family and strategic therapists offer encouragement to (1) be flexible and maneuverable in the ways we position ourselves in relation to the client (Fisch, Weakland, & Segal, 1982); (2) be playful, spontaneous, dramatic, and intuitive during sessions (Satir & Baldwin, 1983); (3) use whatever the client presents in his symptoms, behavior, or resistance as the leverage to initiate change (Erickson, 1964); (4) continue trying other techniques when something fails to work (Bandler & Grinder, 1979); (5) free yourself of the constraints of needing to be correct and give yourself permission to be ineffective until you can find something that does work (Minuchin & Fishman, 1981); (6) do what feels right at the time (Napier & Whitaker, 1978); (7) understand client symptoms as creative solutions to their problems (Madanes, 1990); (8) emphasize the postive aspects rather than exclusively the problematic nature of client experiences (O'Hanlon & Weiner-Davis, 1989); and (9) appreciate the absurdity of human dilemmas and the paradoxes of life, treating symptoms in a similar context (Haley, 1984).

When these cries for intuition and creativity are combined with our natural heritage of empiricism, philosophical inquiry, and the rigorous applications of scientific methodology, we have at our disposal a process that is both creative and cautious, radical and responsible. Clients come to us only after they have already exhausted the more traditional and obvious problem-solving strategies. They have discovered that drugs do not work for very long. Nor does blaming others or wishing that problems would magically vanish. Hiding under the covers feels safe until you have to change the sheets. Faced with nowhere else to go, all other options eliminated, they walk into the therapist's office, defeated. Obviously the cure will be found in something the client has not yet tried or, in the case of very difficult clients, in what no other therapist has yet discovered.

Creative Thinking

In an essay for researchers on breaking out of their conceptual ruts and away from the tendency to think as clones of one another, Wicker (1985) offers some advice that may be applied with equal usefulness to the fostering of creativity in therapists.

1. A playful, whimsical attitude can be adopted by exploring unusual metaphors.
2. A therapist should constantly tinker with the assumptions of her operating principles, especially those she holds most sacred.
3. She should also attempt to expose hidden assumptions by increasing awareness of implicit processes in her work.

The therapist functions much of the time as a detective. First, she attempts to figure out the crime a client feels he has committed that is bad enough to warrant symptomatic punishment. She interviews the suspect, reconstructs the crime, and carefully gathers evidence. She formulates a motive, a hypothesis regarding how and why the symptoms appeared. She deduces a modus operandi, a signature to the crime, a pattern in which the current symptoms fit the client's characteristic style. She gently interrogates the client, squeezing out a confession that will exhaust the need for continued self-punishment. In these activities it is the therapist's willingness to enter the client's world, to sift through all the information available, and, finally, to connect events and intuitively interpret their meaning that will solve the problem. To accomplish these tasks, the therapist must be a creative detective, must be able to see beyond the obvious, to the often disguised and subtle clues that lie embedded in a client's behavior.

Doing Therapy as a Creative Enterprise

There are essentially two points of view in practicing therapy. One approach emphasizes reliability and consistency in interventions. To miminize chance variables and maximize intentionality, Kagan (1973) feels it is crucial for therapists to be able to replicate what they do. When you find something that works—a particular anecdote or metaphor, a structure or intervention, an interpretation or technique— you should, according to this approach, use it again and again. To not do so is to cheat the client of a well-tested remedy that is known to be effective.

For example, one standard and reliable response to the client complaint "I'm not getting any better" is "Then the therapy must be working since it is helping you to become uncomfortable and therefore more motivated to change." Relying on this well-worn intervention may be consistently effective, but in time the therapist begins to feel like a computer that spits out a canned answer to any given button that is pushed.

Some dedicated and very successful therapists do not mind sacrificing their own fresh involvement in the spontaneous process of change for the sake of telling a client something he has told a hundred people. A psychoanalyst explained his rationale for not altering his therapeutic formula: "Look, I've worked a long time to perfect my favorite metaphors. I have no right to exchange them for as-yet-unproven examples just for my own amusement. Of course I get tired of saying the same things to all my clients; but that's what I'm paid to do."

The other point of view conceives of each therapy session as an individual masterpiece. It may, and probably will, contain elements in common with many other works of art in the same style. The same themes repeat themselves. Basically the process of change follows a predictable pattern, even if the client's individual history and the therapist's characteristic style vary. Such a clinician attempts to translate her energy authentically in every session, to create each therapeutic masterpiece with personalized appeal. In the words of one practitioner: "I have this rule never to repeat myself, or at least not in the precise way I expressed something before. If I don't alter the story, I will tell it in a different way or relate it more specifically to the life of a particular client. I have this fantasy that my clients might someday compare notes about what I told them. I can't stand the idea that they might discover I told them the same thing. It is much harder on me to stay on my toes and think of new ways to get points across, but it's worth it: I'm always learning and getting better, and I don't get bored."

The practice of therapy can indeed be an exercise in creativity—especially in the ways we play with language. We are playwrights in that we spontaneously compose and direct dialogue, acting out various roles of a nurturer, an authority, or a character from a client's life. We are poets in that we create images and metaphors to illustrate ideas. Over the years most practitioners have compiled in their heads a wonderful library of helping stories and therapeutic anecdotes they have borrowed or invented. These represent the sum total of a practitioner's life's work. One of the things we do so well as we walk through life is collect things that may be useful in a session at a later time.

Since creativity is essentially the discovery of an analogy on multiple planes that nobody has seen before, therapists are original thinkers of the first order. Take wit and humor as examples. Freud long had an appreciation for humor and a use for wit, not just as another entry into the unconscious but as the highest expression of creativity. Therapists use humor and parody to defuse tension with a client, to confront the client in a less threatening way, or to discuss taboo subjects that might be more difficult to approach from a more direct angle. Implicit in a humorous anecdote or pun could be the nucleus of a major insight, one the client may first laugh at before considering the painful truth the punch line contains.

Laughter, we know, has a cathartic value of its own. The therapist's occasional role as a court jester who seeks to coax a smile out of the frozen features of despair represents only one way humor can be used in the therapeutic process. Koestler (1964, pp. 91–92) found humor to be the best single example of how the creative mind works: "To cause surprise the humorist must have a modicum of originality— the ability to break away from the stereotyped routines of thought. Caricaturist, satirist, the writer of nonsense-humor, and even the expert tickler, each operates on more than one plane. Whether his purpose is to convey a social message, or merely to entertain, he must provide mental jolts, caused by the collision of incompatible matrices."

The preceding theory of humor could also be a description of therapy itself—helping people to break away from stereotyped routines, providing mental jolts, and especially encouraging thinking on multiple levels. In this routine the therapist is a scholar and practitioner of originality par excellence. Each and every client presents us with her perception of a life-threatening crisis or a serious problem that has no solution. Because we are capable of viewing any behavior on many levels, we do not experience the same feelings of being stuck as the client does. We can reframe the problem in a different light, change its shape in such a way that it may more easily be solved. Often, this simple maneuver of looking at the same old problem from a different angle is sufficient in itself to provide immediate relief.

Not only can a therapist's playfulness make a profound difference in energizing our own approach to therapy but it can make a gigantic difference with clients who are stuck. Waters (1992) cautions that although in its right time, place, and circumstances "play lubricates the process of change" (p. 40), it can also be distracting at best and dangerous at worst when it is employed according to the therapist's whim.

Originality is evidenced in the therapist's thinking and behavior in other ways as well. When we stop to consider the conditions likely to spawn creative acts—that is, permissiveness, absence of external criticism, openness to new experience, acceptance of novelty, an emphasis on internal control and individual autonomy, flexible problem solving, integration of cognitive / affective dimensions, psychological safety and support—we realize we are describing the experience of therapy (Rogers, [1954] 1978). The client and the therapist interact within an environment that is designed to promote the maximum amount of creative thinking. Each gives the other permission to experiment with new ideas and novel approaches to problem solving. The client is encouraged to consider unusual ways of looking at her life, her goals, and the methods of getting where she wants to be. All the while a client is attempting to go beyond previously defined limits and choices, the therapist is busy processing all the information that has been presented: past history, current functioning, complaints and symptoms, and interaction style are collated in the brain until finally there is a startling moment of revelation. By combining all the data in a unique and organized way, a creative interpretation of the client's behavior is invented. Further innovation is required to determine the best way to facilitate the client's insights and, later, to help her act on the knowledge in a constructive manner.

For those therapists who value creativity in their work, innovative strategies become second nature. More importantly, such therapists become less certain of what they already know. For centuries helping professionals were absolutely certain that the mentally afflicted were possessed with demons that needed to be exorcised. It is arrogance of the intellect that has drawn us into the Dark Ages. Those therapists who are possessed with the single-minded devotion to a way of doing things, without consideration for revision and evolution, will hardly advance the state of our profession.

Creative therapists listen to the voice inside them. They pay attention to what does not make sense, even though things may have always been done that way. They are constructive rule breakers. They take cases that make them feel uncomfortable. They treat each case as if it were unique. And most of all, they enjoy the company of other people who challenge their ideas. They find their creativity nurtured in their interactions with colleagues and especially with clients.

The mutual creative energy fostered in the client and therapist as they encounter one another is a final factor in the chain of consequences that are part of their reciprocal influence. For Bugental (1978) being a therapist is much more than making a buck or belonging to a prestigious profession. It is "an arena for my creativity and endless raw material to feed it. It has been the source of anguish, pain, and anxiety—sometimes in the work itself, but more frequently within myself and with those important in my life in confrontations stimulated directly or indirectly by the impact of the work and relationships with my clients" (pp. 149–150). For Bugental (1976) being a creative therapist involves the process of becoming more aware. It is not necessary for us to do anything to ourselves, to change anything in our lives, to alter our style of helping. Rather, we can be more aware of ourselves just as we are. This process involves recovering our own vision that has become unduly influenced by our mentors and not influenced enough by our own experiences.

Our clients do indeed change us almost as much as we change them. Even though we know, understand, and enforce the rules and guard against infection by clients, and even though they are amateurs at influence, befuddled and distracted as they are with their own concerns, we cannot remain completely unaffected. We are touched by their goodness and the joy and privilege we feel in being allowed to get so close to a human soul. And we are harmed by their malicious and destructive energy. Whenever we enter a room with another life in great torment, we will find no escape from our own despair. And we will find no way to hold down the elation we feel as a witness to another person's transformation — just as we are the catalyst for our own.

references

Alexander, F. G., & Selesnick, S. T. (1966). *The history of psychiatry*. New York: Mentor.

Anderson, C. (1987, May/June). The crisis of priorities. *Family Therapy Networker*, pp. 19–25.

Anthony, C. P., & Thibodeau, G. A. (1979). *Textbook of anatomy and physiology*. St. Louis, MO: Mosby.

Bach, G. (1979). The George Bach self-recognition inventory for burned-out therapists. *Voices, 15*, 73–77.

Bandler, R., & Grinder, J. (1979). *Frogs into princes*. Moab, UT: Real People Press.

Bandura, A. (1977). *Social learning theory*. Englewood Cliffs, NJ: Prentice-Hall.

Basecu, S. (1990). Tools of the trade: The use of self in psychotherapy. *Group, 14*, 157–165.

Bellack, L., & Faithorn, P. (1981). *Crises and special problems in psychoanalysis and psychotherapy*. New York: Brunner/Mazel.

Belson, R. (1992, September/October). Therapist burnout. *Family Therapy Networker*, p. 22.

Bermak, G. E. (1977). Do psychiatrists have special emotional problems? *American Journal of Psychoanalysis*, *37*, 141–146.

Beutler, L. E. (1983). *Eclectic psychotherapy: A systematic approach*. Elmsford, NY: Pergamon Press.

Bloom, M. (1975). *The paradox of helping*. New York: Wiley.

Boorstein, D. (1983). *The discoverers*. New York: Random House.

Boy, A. V., & Pine, G. J. (1982). *Client-centered counseling: A renewal*. Needham Heights, MA: Allyn & Bacon.

Breuer, G. (1982). *Sociobiology and the human dimension*. Cambridge, England: Cambridge University Press.

Bronowski, J. (1978). *The origins of knowledge and imagination*. New Haven, CT: Yale University Press.

Bugental, J.F.T. (1976). *The search for existential identity: Patient-therapist dialogues in humanistic psychotherapy*. San Francisco: Jossey-Bass.

Bugental, J.F.T. (1978). *Psychotherapy and process*. Reading, MA: Addison-Wesley.

Bugental, J.F.T. (1990). *Intimate journeys: Stories from life-changing therapy*. San Francisco: Jossey-Bass.

Bugental, J.F.T. (1991). Lessons clients teach therapists. *Journal of Humanistic Psychology*, *31*, 28–32.

Burton, A. (1972). Healing as a lifestyle. In A. Burton & Associates (Eds.), *Twelve therapists: How they live and actualize themselves*. San Francisco: Jossey-Bass.

Campbell, K. (1982). The psychotherapy relationship with borderline personality disorders. *Psychotherapy: Theory, Research, and Practice*, *19*, 166–193.

Carroll, L. (1981). *Through the looking-glass*. New York: Bantam Books. (Originally published 1871.)

Castaneda, C. A. (1971). *A separate reality*. New York: Simon & Schuster.

Caughey, J. L. (1978, September). Media mentors. *Psychology Today*, pp. 44–49.

Cerney, M. S. (1985). Countertransference revisited. *Journal of Counseling and Development*, *63*, 362–364.

Chessick, R. (1978). The sad soul of the psychiatrist. *Bulletin of the Menninger Clinic*, *42*(1), 1–10.

Clark, J. Z. (1991). Therapist narcissism. *Professional Psychology: Research and Practice*, *22*, 141–143.

Colson, D. B., Allen, J. G., Coyne, L., Dexter, N., Jehl, N., Mayer, C. A., & Spohn, H. (1986). An anatomy of countertransference: Staff reactions to difficult psychiatric hospital patients. *Hospital and Community Psychiatry*, *37*, 923–928.

Combs, A. V., Avila, D. L., & Purkey, W. W. (1971). *Helping relationships*. Needham Heights, MA: Allyn & Bacon.

Coombs, R. H., & Fawzy, F. I. (1986). The impaired-physician syndrome: A developmental perspective. In C. D. Scott & J. Hawk (Eds.), *Heal thyself: The health of health care professionals*. New York: Brunner/Mazel.

Corey, G. (1991). *Theory and practice of counseling and psychotherapy* (4th ed.). Pacific Grove, CA: Brooks/Cole.

Corey, G., Corey, M. S., & Callanan, P. (1988). *Issues and ethics in the helping professions.* Pacific Grove, CA: Brooks/Cole.

Corey, M. S., & Corey, G. (1993). *Becoming a helper* (2nd ed.). Pacific Grove, CA: Brooks/Cole.

Csikszentmihalyi, M. (1975). *Beyond boredom and anxiety: The experience of play in work and games.* San Francisco: Jossey-Bass.

Csikszentmihalyi, M. (1990). *Flow: The psychology of optimal experience.* New York: HarperCollins.

Cunningham, S. (1985, May). Rollo May: The case for love, beauty, and the humanities. *APA Monitor*, p. 17.

Curtis, J. M. (1982). The effect of therapist self-disclosure on patients' perceptions of empathy, competence, and trust in an analogue psychotherapeutic interaction. *Psychotherapy: Theory, Research, and Practice, 19*(1), 54–62.

Dai, B. (1979). My experience of psychotherapy. *Voices, 15*(2), 26–33.

Decker, R. J. (1988). *Effective psychotherapy: The silent dialogue.* New York: Hemisphere.

Derlega, V. J., Hendrick, S. S., Winstead, B. A., & Berg, J. H. (1991). *Psychotherapy as a personal relationship.* New York: Guilford.

de Shazer, S. (1988). *Clues: Investigating solutions in brief therapy.* New York: W.W.Norton.

Deutsch, C. J. (1984). Self-reported sources of stress among psychotherapists. *Professional Psychology: Research and Practice, 15*, 833–845.

Deutsch, C. J. (1985). A survey of therapists' personal problems and treatment. *Professional Psychology: Research and Practice*, *16*, 305–315.

Donleavy, J. P. (1975). *The unexpurgated code*. New York: Delta.

Dorn, F. J. (1984, February). The social influence model: A social psychological approach to counseling. *Personnel and Guidance Journal*, pp. 342–345.

Dyer, W. W., & Vriend, J. (1977). *Counseling techniques that work*. Ramsey, NJ: Funk & Wagnalls.

Edelwich, J., & Brodsky, A. (1980). *Burn-out*. New York: Human Sciences Press.

Elkind, S. N. (1992). *Resolving impasses in therapeutic relationships*. New York: Guilford.

Ellis, A. (1972). Psychotherapy without tears. In A. Burton & Associates (Eds.), *Twelve therapists: How they live and actualize themselves*. San Francisco: Jossey-Bass.

Ellis, A. (1983). Article. *Psychotherapy in Private Practice*, *1*(1).

Ellis, A. (1984). How to deal with your most difficult client—you. *Psychotherapy in Private Practice*, *1984*; *2*(1), 25–34.

English, O. S. (1972). How I found my way to psychiatry. In A. Burton & Associates (Eds.), *Twelve therapists: How they live and actualize themselves*. San Francisco: Jossey-Bass.

Erickson, M. (1964). An hypnotic technique for resistant patients. *American Journal of Clinical Hypnosis*, *1*, 8–32.

Erikson, E. (1963). *Childhood and society*. New York: W.W.Norton.

Farber, B. A. (1983a). The effects of psychotherapeutic practice upon psychotherapists. *Psychotherapy: Theory, Research, and Practice, 20*(2), 174–182.

Farber, B. A. (1983b). Psychotherapists' perceptions of stressful patient behavior. *Professional Psychology: Research and Practice, 15*, 833–845.

Farber, B. A., & Heifetz, L. J. (1981). The satisfaction and stress of psychotherapeutic work. *Professional Psychology, 12*, 621–630.

Fine, H. J. (1980). Despair and depletion in the therapist. *Psychotherapy: Theory, Research, and Practice, 17*(4), 392–395.

Fine, R. (1972). Search for love. In A. Burton & Associates (Eds.), *Twelve therapists: How they live and actualize themselves*. San Francisco: Jossey-Bass.

Fisch, R., Weakland, J. H., & Segal, L. (1982). *The tactics of change: Doing therapy briefly*. San Francisco: Jossey-Bass.

Fish, J. M. (1973). *Placebo therapy: A practical guide to social influence in psychotherapy*. San Francisco: Jossey-Bass.

Fisher, K. (1985). Charges catch clinicians in cycle of shame, slip ups. *APA Monitor, 16*(5), 6–7.

Fitzgerald, F. S. (1933). *Tender is the night*. New York: Charles Scribner's Sons.

Frank, J. D. (1961). *Persuasion and healing*. New York: Schocken.

Frank, R. (1979). Money and other trade-offs in psychotherapy. *Voices, 14*(4), 42–44.

Freud, A. (1954). The widening scope of indication for psychoanalysis. *Journal of American Psychoanalytic Association, 2,* 607–620.

Freud, S. (1912). The dynamics of transference. In *Collected Papers, Vol. 8.* London: Imago.

Freud, S. (1950). Analysis: Terminable or interminable. In *Collected Papers, Vol. 5.* London: Hogarth Press. (Originally published 1937.)

Freud, S. (1954). *The origins of psychoanalysis.* New York: Basic Books. (Originally published 1897.)

Freud, S. (1955). Letter to Ferenczi, Oct. 6, 1910. In E. Jones, *The life and work of Sigmund Freud, Vol. 2.* New York: Basic Books.

Freudenberger, H. J. (1975). The staff burn-out syndrome in alternative institutions. *Psychotherapy: Theory, Research, and Practice, 12*(1), 73–82.

Freudenberger, H. J. (1986). The health professional in treatment: Symptoms, dynamics, and treatment issues. In C. D. Scott & J. Hawk (Eds.), *Heal thyself: The health of health care professionals.* New York: Brunner / Mazel.

Gilbert, P., Hughes, W., & Dryden, W. (1989). The therapist as a crucial variable in psychotherapy. In W. Dryden & L. Spurling (Eds.), *On becoming a psychotherapist.* London: Tavistock / Routledge.

Gordon, D. (1978). *Therapeutic metaphors.* Cupertino, CA: Meta Publications.

Griswell, G. E. (1979). Dead tired and bone weary. *Voices*, *152*, 49–53.

Gross, D., & Kahn, J. (1983). Values of three practitioner groups. *Journal of Counseling and Values*, *28*(1), 228–333.

Guy, J. D. (1987). *The personal life of the psychotherapist*. New York: Wiley.

Guy, J. D., Poelstra, P. L., & Stark, M. J. (1988). Personal distress and therapeutic effectiveness. *Professional Psychology: Research and Practice*, *20*, 48–50.

Guy, J. D., Stark, M., & Poelstra, P. (1987). *National survey of psychotherapists' attitudes and beliefs*. Unpublished manuscript.

Haley, J. (1973). *Uncommon therapy*. New York: W.W.Norton.

Haley, J. (1984). *Ordeal therapy: Unusual ways to change behavior*. San Francisco: Jossey-Bass.

Haley, J. (1987). *Problem-solving therapy* (2nd ed.). San Francisco: Jossey-Bass.

Haley, J. (1989). *The first therapy session* (audiotape). San Francisco: Jossey-Bass.

Harrison, J. (1984). *Sundog*. New York: Dutton.

Hayward, J. W. (1984). *Perceiving ordinary magic*. Boulder, CO: New Science Library.

Healy, S. D. (1984). *Boredom, self, and culture*. Madison, NJ: Fairleigh Dickinson University Press.

Henry, W. E. (1966). Some observations on the lives of healers. *Human Development*, *9*, 47–56.

Henry, W. E., Sims, J. H., & Spray, S. L. (1973). *Public and private lives of psychotherapists*. San Francisco: Jossey-Bass.

Herlihy, B., & Corey, G. (1992). *Dual relationships in counseling*. Alexandria, VA: American Counseling Association.

Herron, W. G., & Rouslin, S. (1984). *Issues in psychotherapy*. Washington, DC: Oryn Publications.

Herron, W. G., & Welt, S. R. (1992). *Money matters: The role of the fee in psychotherapy and psychoanalysis*. New York: Guilford.

Hobson, R. F. (1985). *Forms of feeling: The heart of psychotherapy*. London: Tavistock/Routledge.

Holroyd, J. C., & Brodsky, A. M. (1977). Psychologists' attitudes and practices regarding erotic and nonerotic physical contact with patients. *American Psychologist*, *32*, 843–849.

Jourard, S. M. (1971). *The transparent self*. New York: Van Nostrand Reinhold.

Kagan, N. (1973). Can technology help us toward reliability in influencing human interaction? In J. Vriend & W. W. Dyer (Eds.), *Counseling effectively in groups*. Englewood Cliffs, NJ: Educational Technology.

Keen, S. (1977, May). Boredom and how to beat it. *Psychology Today*, pp. 78–84.

Keeney, B. P. (1991). *Improvisational therapy*. New York: Guilford.

Kellerman, J. (1992). *Private eyes*. New York: Bantam.

Kennedy, R. S., & Reeves, P. (Eds.). (1970). *The notebooks of Thomas Wolfe*. Chapel Hill: University of North Carolina Press. (Originally published 1921.)

Kennedy, W. (1983). *Ironweed*. New York: Viking Penguin.

Keyes, R. (1985). *Chancing it: Why we take risks*. Boston: Little, Brown.

Kierkegaard, S. (1944). *Either/or*. Princeton, NJ: Princeton University Press.

Klopfer, W. G. (1974). The seductive patient. In W. G. Klopfer & M. R. Reed (Eds.), *Problems in psychotherapy*. New York: Wiley.

Koestler, A. (1964). *The act of creation*. New York: Dell.

Kopp, S. (1972). *If you meet the Buddha on the road, kill him!* Palo Alto, CA: Science and Behavior Books, 1972.

Kopp, S. (1985). *Even a stone can be a teacher*. Los Angeles: Tarcher, 1985.

Kottler, J. A. (1983). *Pragmatic group leadership*. Pacific Grove, CA: Brooks/Cole.

Kottler, J. A. (1990). *Private moments, secret selves: Enriching our time alone*. New York: Ballantine.

Kottler, J. A. (1991). *The compleat therapist*. San Francisco: Jossey-Bass.

Kottler, J. A. (1992a). *Compassionate therapy: Working with difficult clients*. San Francisco: Jossey-Bass.

Kottler, J. A. (1992b). Confronting our own hypocrisy: Being a model for our students and clients. *Journal of Counseling and Development*, 70, 475–476.

Kottler, J. A. (1993). *Advanced group leadership*. Pacific Grove, CA: Brooks/Cole.

Kottler, J. A., & Blau, D. S. (1989). *The imperfect therapist: Learning from failure in therapeutic practice*. San Francisco: Jossey-Bass.

Kottler, J. A., & Brown, R. W. (1992). *Introduction to therapeutic counseling* (2nd ed.). Pacific Grove, CA: Brooks/Cole.

Kovacs, A. L. (1976). The emotional hazards of teaching psychotherapy. *Psychotherapy: Theory, Research, and Practice*, *13*(4), 321–334.

Kramer, R., & Weiner, I. (1983, November). Psychiatry on the borderline. *Psychotherapy Today*, pp. 70–73.

Lamb, F. B. (1971). *Wizard of the upper Amazon*. Boston: Houghton Mifflin.

Levinson, D. (1978). *The seasons of a man's life*. New York: Knopf.

London, P. (1985). *The modes and morals of psychotherapy* (2nd ed.). New York: Hemisphere.

Looney, J. G., Harding, R. K., Blotcky, M. J., & Barnhart, F. D. (1980). Psychiatrists' transition from training to career: Stress and mastery. *American Journal of Psychiatry*, *137*, 32–35.

Lowen, A. (1983). *Narcissism*. New York: Macmillan.

Luks, A. (1988). Helper's high. *Psychology Today*, Oct., 39–42.

McConnaughy, E. A. (1987). The person of the therapist in psychotherapeutic practice. *Psychotherapy*, *24*, 303–314.

Madanes, C. (1981). *Strategic family therapy*. San Francisco: Jossey-Bass.

Madanes, C. (1990). *Metaphors and paradoxes* (audiotape). San Francisco: Jossey-Bass.

Maeder, T. (1989, January.). Wounded healers. *The Atlantic Monthly*, pp. 37–47.

Mahoney, M. J., & Eiseman, S. C. (1989). The object of the dance. In W. Dryden & L. Spurling (Eds.), *On becoming a psychotherapist*. London: Tavistock/Routledge.

Mahrer, A. R. (1989). *The integration of psychotherapies*. New York: Human Sciences Press.

Mahrer, A. R., & Morel, C. (1993). How to become an even better counselor than you are now. *The Guidepost, 35*(9).

Martin, E. S., & Schurtman, R. (1985). Termination anxiety as it affects the therapist. *Psychotherapy: Theory, Research, and Practice, 22*(1), 92–96.

Maslach, C. (1982). *Burnout: The cost of caring*. Englewood Cliffs, NJ: Prentice-Hall.

Maslach, C. (1986). Stress, burnout, and workaholism. In R. R. Kilburg, P. E. Nathan, & R. W. Thoreson (Eds.), *Professionals in distress*. Washington, DC: American Psychological Association.

Maslow, A. (1968). *Toward a psychology of being*. New York: Van Nostrand Reinhold.

Masterson, J. F. (1983). *Countertransference and psychotherapeutic technique*. New York: Brunner/Mazel.

May, R. (1958). *Existence*. New York: Simon & Schuster.

May, R. (1975). *The courage to create*. New York: W.W.Norton.

May, R. (1983). *The discovery of being*. New York: W.W.Norton.

Mellan, O. (1992, March/April). The last taboo. *Family Therapy Networker*, pp. 40–47.

Miller, A. (1981). *The drama of the gifted child.* New York: Basic Books.

Millon, T., Millon, C., & Antoni, M. (1986). Sources of emotional and mental disorders among psychologists: A career perspective. In R. R. Kilburg, P. E. Nathan, & R. W. Thoreson (Eds.), *Professionals in distress.* Washington, DC: American Psychological Association.

Minuchin, S., & Fishman, H. C. (1981). *Family therapy techniques.* Cambridge, MA: Harvard University Press.

Morgan, W. P. (1978, April). The mind of the marathoner. *Psychology Today*, pp. 38–47.

Moss, R. (1981). *The I that is we.* Berkeley, CA: Celestial Arts.

Napier, A. Y., & Whitaker, C. A. (1978). *The family crucible.* New York: Bantam.

Nash, J., Norcross, J. C., & Prochaska, J. O. (1984). Satisfaction and stresses of independent practice. *Psychotherapy in Private Practice, 2*(4), 39–48.

Nathan, P. E. (1986). Unanswered questions about distressed professionals. In R. R. Kilburg, P. E. Nathan, & R. W. Thoreson (Eds.), *Professionals in distress.* Washington, DC: American Psychological Association.

Natterson, J. (1991). *Beyond countertransference.* Northvale, NJ: Jason Aronson.

Norcross, J. C., & Guy, J. D. (1989). Ten therapists: The process of becoming and being. In W. Dryden & L. Spurling (Eds.), *On becoming a psychotherapist.* London: Tavistock/Routledge.

Norcross, J. C., & Prochaska, J. O. (1986). Psychotherapist heal thyself: The psychological distress and self-change of psychologists, counselors, and laypersons. *Psychotherapy, 23*, 102–114.

O'Hanlon, W. H., & Weiner-Davis, M. (1989). *In search of solutions.* New York: W.W.Norton.

Otani, A. (1989). Client resistance in counseling: Its theoretical rationale and taxonomic classification. *Journal of Counseling and Development, 67*, 458–461.

Palmer, J. O. (1980). *A primer of eclectic psychotherapy.* Pacific Grove, CA: Brooks/Cole.

Patterson, C. H. (1985). What is the placebo in psychotherapy? *Psychotherapy: Theory, Research, and Practice, 22*(2), 163–169.

Peck, M. S. (1978). *The road less traveled.* New York: Simon & Schuster.

Penzer, W. N. (1984). The psychopathology of the psychotherapist. *Psychotherapy in Private Practice, 2*(2), 51–59.

Perry, M. A., & Furukawa, J. M. (1980). Modeling methods. In F. H. Kanfer & A. P. Goldstein (Eds.), *Helping people change.* Elmsford, NY: Pergamon Press.

Pines, A. M., Aronson, E., & Kafry, D. (1981). *Burnout.* New York: Free Press.

Pittman, F. (1992, January/February). It's not my fault. *Family Therapy Networker*, pp. 57–63.

Polster, E. (1972). Stolen by gypsies. In A. Burton & Associates (Eds.), *Twelve therapists: How they live and actualize themselves.* San Francisco: Jossey-Bass.

Pope, K. S., & Bouhoutsos, J. C. (1986). *Sexual intimacy between therapists and patients*. New York: Praeger.

Pope, K. S., Keith-Spiegel, P., & Tabachnick, B. G. (1986). Sexual attraction to clients. *American Psychologists*, *41*(2), 147–156.

Pope, K. S., & Vasquez, M.J.T. (1991). *Ethics in psychotherapy and counseling: A practical guide for psychologists*. San Francisco: Jossey-Bass.

Rainer, T. (1978). *The new diary*. Los Angeles: Tarcher.

Ram Dass & Gorman, P. (1985). *How can I help? Stories and reflections on service*. New York: Knopf.

Rice, P. L. (1992). *Stress and health* (2nd ed.). Pacific Grove, CA: Brooks/Cole.

Rippere, V., & Williams, R. (Eds.). *Wounded healers*. New York: Wiley.

Robbins, J. M., Beck, P. R., Mueller, D. P., & Mizener, D. A. (1988). Therapists' perceptions of difficult psychiatric patients. *Journal of Nervous and Mental Diseases*, *176*, 490–496.

Robbins, T. (1980). *Still life with woodpecker*. New York: Bantam Books.

Rogers, C. (1972). My personal growth. In A. Burton & Associates (Eds.), *Twelve therapists: How they live and actualize themselves*. San Francisco: Jossey-Bass.

Rogers, C. R. (1978). Toward a theory of creativity. In A. Rothenberg & C. R. Hausman (Eds.), *The creativity question*. Durham, NC: Duke University Press. (Originally published 1954.)

de Saint-Exupéry, A. (1943). *The little prince*. Orlando, FL: Harcourt Brace Jovanovich.

Satir, V., & Baldwin, M. (1983). *Satir step by step*. Palo Alto, CA: Science and Behavior Books.

Schneiderman, S. (1983). *Jacques Lacan: The death of an intellectual hero*. Cambridge, MA: Harvard University Press.

Schön, D. A. (1983). *The reflective practitioner*. New York: Basic Books.

Schor, J. B. (1992, March/April). Work, spend, work, spend: Is this any way to live? *Family Therapy Networker*, pp. 24–25.

Shepard, M. A. (1972). *Inside a psychiatrist's head*. New York: Dell.

Silverstein, S. (1964). *The giving tree*. New York: HarperCollins.

Sinclair, J. D. (1982, November). How the mind recharges batteries. *Psychology Today*, p. 96.

Singer, J. L., Sincoff, J. B., & Kolligian, J. (1989). Counter-transference and cognition: Studying the psychotherapist's distortions as consequences of normal information processing. *Psychotherapy*, *26*, 344–355.

Smith, A. (1976, April). The benefits of boredom. *Psychology Today*, pp. 46–51.

Spense, D. P. (1982). *Narrative and historical truth*. New York: W.W.Norton.

Spurling, L., & Dryden, W. (1989). The self and the therapeutic domain. In W. Dryden & L. Spurling (Eds.), *On becoming a psychotherapist*. London: Tavistock/Routledge.

Stadler, H. A. (1990). Counselor impairment. In B. Herlihy

& L. B. Golden (Eds.), *Ethical standards casebook* (4th ed.). Alexandria, VA: American Counseling Association.

Stein, H. (1982). *Ethics and other liabilities*. New York: St. Martin's Press.

Steinzor, B. (1972). Mystery of self and other. In A. Burton & Associates (Eds.), *Twelve therapists: How they live and actualize themselves*. San Francisco: Jossey-Bass.

Strong, S. (1982). Emerging integrations of clinical and social psychology: A clinician's perspective. In G. Weary & H. Mirels (Eds.), *Integrations of clinical and social psychology*. New York: Oxford University Press.

Strupp, H. H. (1980). Humanism and psychotherapy: A personal statement of the therapist's essential values. *Psychotherapy: Theory, Research, and Practice, 17*(4), 396–400.

Thomas, L. (1974). *The medusa and the snail*. New York: Viking Penguin.

Thoreson, R. W., Budd, F. C., & Krauskopf, C. J. (1986). Perceptions of alcohol misuse and work behavior among professionals: Identification and intervention. *Professional Psychology: Research and Practice, 17*, 210–216.

Thoreson, R. W., Miller, M., & Krauskopf, C. J. (1989). The distressed psychologist: Prevalence and treatment considerations. *Professional Psychology: Research and Practice, 20*, 153–158.

Van Hoose, W. H., & Kottler, J. A. (1985). *Ethical and legal issues in counseling and psychotherapy: A comprehensive guide* (2nd ed.). San Francisco: Jossey-Bass.

Viscott, D. (1977). *Risking*. New York: Pocket Books.

Vriend, J., & Dyer, W. W. (1973). *Counseling for personal mastery* (audiotape series). Washington, DC: Association for Counseling and Development Press.

Wakeling, P. (1985). Awakenings by a consultant psychiatrist. In V. Riperre & R. Williams (Eds.), *Wounded healers*. New York: Wiley.

Warkentin, J. (1972). Paradox of being alien and intimate. In A. Burton & Associates (Eds.), *Twelve therapists: How they live and actualize themselves*. San Francisco: Jossey-Bass.

Waters, D. (1992, September/October). Therapy as an excellent adventure. *Family Therapy Networker*, pp. 38–45.

Watkins, C. E. (1985). Countertransference: Its impact on the counseling situation. *Journal of Counseling and Development, 63*, 356–359.

Weil, A. (1983). *Health and healing*. Boston: Houghton Mifflin.

Weiner, M. F. (1982). *The psychotherapeutic impasse*. New York: Free Press.

Weisman, A. (1973). Confrontation, countertransference, and context. In G. Adler & P. G. Myerson (Eds.), *Confrontation in psychotherapy*. New York: Science House.

Welt, S. R., & Herron, W. G. (1990). *Narcissism and the psychotherapist*. New York: Guilford.

Wicker, A. W. (1985, October). Getting out of Conceptual ruts. *American Psychologist*, pp. 1094–1103.

Wilber, K. (1983). *Eye to eye*. Garden City, NY: Anchor Books.

Wong, N. (1983). Perspectives of the difficult patient. *Bulletin of the Menninger Clinic*, 47, 99–106.

Wood, B., Klein, S., Cross, H. J., Lammes, C. J., & Elliot, J. K. (1985). Impaired practitioners: Psychologists' opinions about prevalence, and proposals for intervention. *Professional Psychology: Research and Practice*, 16, 843–850.

Wylie, M. S., & Markowitz, L. M. (1992, September/October). Walking the wire. *Family Therapy Networker*, pp. 19–30.

Yalom, I. D. (1980). *Existential psychotherapy*. New York: Basic Books.

Yalom, I. D. (1989). *Love's executioner and other tales of psychotherapy*. New York: Basic Books.

Zelen, S. L. (1985). Sexualization of therapeutic relationships: The dual vulnerability of patient and therapist. *Psychotherapy: Theory, Research, and Practice*, 22(2), 178–185.

index